BRITISH STEAM
LOCOMOTIVES

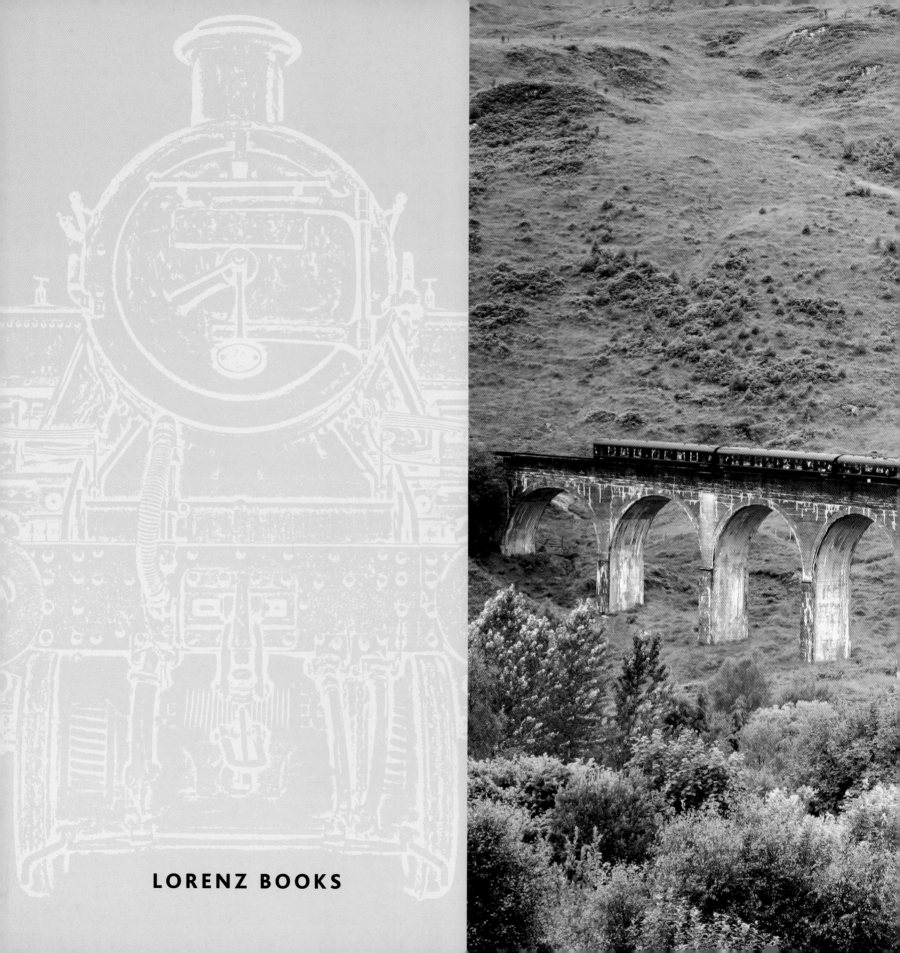

LORENZ BOOKS

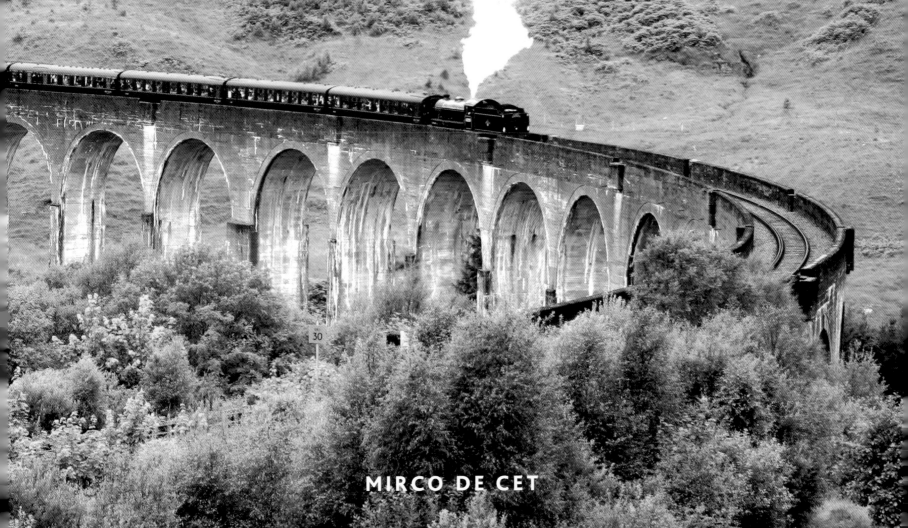

BRITISH STEAM
LOCOMOTIVES

THE STEAM TRAINS OF GREAT BRITAIN SHOWN IN 200 PHOTOGRAPHS

MIRCO DE CET

This edition is published by Lorenz Books,
an imprint of Anness Publishing Ltd

info@anness.com

www.lorenzbooks.com;
www.annesspublishing.com;

Anness Publishing has a new picture agency outlet for images for publishing, promotions
or advertising. Please visit our website www.practicalpictures.com for more information.

A CIP catalogue record for this book
is available from the British Library.

Publisher: Joanna Lorenz
Senior Editor: Felicity Forster
Produced for Anness Publishing Ltd by Editorial Developments,
Edgmond, Shropshire, England
Designer: Chensie Chen
Production: Ben Worley

PUBLISHER'S NOTE
Although the information in this book is believed to be accurate and true at the
time of going to press, neither the authors nor the publisher can accept any legal
responsibility or liability for any errors or omissions that may have been made.

Contents

Getting on Track

Even as early as 1689, English engineer Thomas Savery had created a steam engine which was used to pump water from the mines in Cornwall, England. By 1712, Thomas Newcomen, another English engineer, developed an improved version. But it was the Scottish inventor and mechanical engineer James Watt who made the most significant improvements, which allowed steam engines to be used in a variety of industrial situations, rather than just pumping water from mines. The steam engine could now be adapted for use in many other areas such as steamboats and railroads.

The idea of running carts in tracks carved into rock dates back at least as far as ancient Greece, and wooden-railed wagonways originated in Germany in the 16th century, but the first use of steam locomotives occurred in Great Britain. These early 'railroads' were constructed from parallel rails made of timber on which horses pulled their carts.

Rail technology progressed at an alarming pace, and it was John Birkenshaw who, in 1820, introduced a method of rolling wrought-iron rails, which would be used as a standard for the future.

Richard Trevithick designed and built the first steam locomotive in 1804, and the first commercially successful steam locomotive was the Salamanca, built in 1812 by John Blenkinsop and Matthew Murray for the 4 ft (1219 mm) gauge Middleton Railway. The first passenger-carrying public railway, though horse-drawn, was the Oystermouth Railway in 1807. In 1813 William Hedley and Timothy Hackworth designed a locomotive known as Puffing Billy, for use on the tramway between Stockton and Darlington, and just one year later George Stephenson improved on that design with his first locomotive, Blücher.

Locomotion No. 1 was built by Robert Stephenson and Company in 1825, and was the vehicle that hauled the first train on the Stockton and Darlington Railway on September 27, 1825.

It was this design that convinced the backers of the proposed Stockton and Darlington Railway to appoint Stephenson as engineer for the line in 1821. The 25 mile (40 km) long route opened on September 27, 1825 and with the aid of Stephenson's Locomotion No. 1, it became the first locomotive-hauled public railway in the world.

These first public railways were built as local rail links operated by small private railway companies. With increasing rapidity, more and more lines were built, until the vast majority of towns and villages had at least one rail connection, and sometimes two or three. The age of steam transportation had truly arrived.

This painting by John Dobbin depicts the official opening of the Stockton and Darlington Railway in 1825. People came from all around to see the first steam-hauled passenger train.

Wagonways were built in England as early as the 16th century. This is an example of an early horse-drawn coal wagon, with wooden rails and wooden wheels.

Puffing Billy was built in 1813–14 by engineer William Hedley, enginewright Jonathan Forster and blacksmith Timothy Hackworth. It is the world's oldest surviving steam locomotive.

The Big Four

During the period 1923–1947, the railways in Great Britain were run by four big companies. World War One had seen the government take charge of the railways, and after the conflict was over, it was agreed that having fewer companies running the railways had its advantages. Under the Railways Act of 1921 almost all of the existing rail companies would be grouped together into four new companies:

- London, Midland and Scottish Railway (LMS)
- Great Western Railway (GWR)
- London and North Eastern Railway (LNER)
- Southern Railway (SR)

A few lines remained outside the jurisdiction of the Big Four: in particular, joint railways such as the Midland and Great Northern Joint Railway, and the Somerset and Dorset Joint Railway.

Although the Big Four were not actually in competition with each other, plenty of sparring went on to show who had the fastest, most comfortable and most modern trains. The abandonment of the agreement between LNER and LMS not to compete on the London to Scotland run led to the steam locomotive's finest hour. Two men, Sir Nigel Gresley and Sir William Stanier, fought a friendly but intense rivalry as they strived to build the fastest steam train in the land.

After World War One, war-surplus vans and lorries were sold off at incredibly low prices. Along with the construction of more and better roads, this had a devastating impact on the railways, as freight and passengers transferred to the newly-constructed highways. In some respects the railways also had their hands tied. They were obliged by government to honour the 'common carrier' requirement, which had been brought in during the 19th century. It obliged railway companies to carry any cargo offered to them at a nationally agreed charge, which was generally below a rate needed to make the operation profitable – the intention being to stop railway companies 'cherry picking' the most profitable freight, while also refusing to carry less profitable freight. But now, with

We have the legendary scrap yard of Woodham Brothers at Barry, South Glamorgan to thank for the many locomotives that now run on our Preserved lines. It was here where most were stored and then bought from.

road competition increasing, it put them at a disadvantage. The railways did try to hit back in the late 1930s, with a national campaign for a 'square deal'. This would allow them the same advantages as the road hauliers, but sadly, just as a positive outcome looked likely, World War Two broke out, and the 'common carrier' requirement remained until 1957.

With more people able to own their own cars and the negative situation with freight and passengers, the Big Four struggled to make any profit. Even so, they invested heavily in the modernization of the lines and new rolling stock – locomotives, coaches and wagons – which had been badly neglected during and immediately after World War One.

During World War Two, the railways were used more extensively than any time in their history, with management of the Big Four working together, creating a single company. Much damage was sustained by the railways during the war years, in particular in London and Coventry, where the German Luftwaffe concentrated their bombing. In 1948 the railways were finally nationalized and amalgamated under British Railways. In the mid-1950s there was talk of extensive modernization, but it was soon realized that many of the rural lines had now outlived their usefulness and that things would have to change. A set of proposals for the future of the railways – the 'Beeching Plan' – was adopted by the government. This resulted in the closure of a third of the rail network and the scrapping of a third of a million freight wagons. The Beeching axe had fallen and another nail had been hammered into the already half-closed coffin of the steam locomotive.

It is incredible to think that such a famous locomotive as the Green Arrow, for example, was parked at the Barry scrap yard, quietly rotting and waiting to be cut up for scrap.

Birth of the LMS

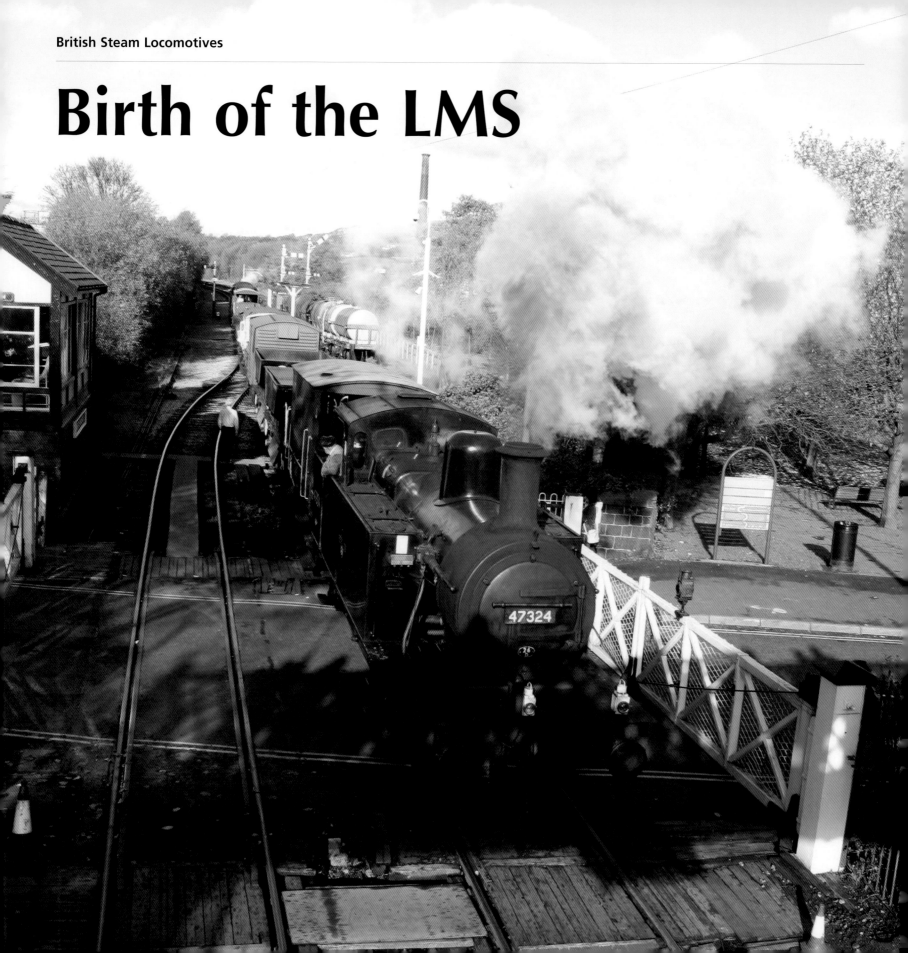

The London, Midland and Scottish Railway (LMS) was formed on January 1,1923 as part of the forced grouping of over 300 separate railway companies into just four.

The LMS was formed from the following major companies:

Caledonian Railway

Furness Railway

Glasgow and South Western Railway

Highland Railway

London and North Western Railway (including the Lancashire and Yorkshire Railway)

Midland Railway

North Staffordshire Railway

There were also some 24 subsidiary railways, leased or worked by the above companies, and a large number of joint railways, along with three railways in Ireland.

The principal LMS trunk routes were the West Coast Main Line and the Midland Main Line, which linked London, the industrial Midlands and the north-west of England, and Scotland. The railways' main business was the transportation of freight between these major industrial centres. Particularly notable were the Toton–Brent coal trains, which took coal from the Nottinghamshire coalfields to London.

The early history of the LMS was dominated by infighting between its two largest constituents, and previously fierce rivals, the Midland and the North Western. Generally, the Midland prevailed, with the adoption of many Midland practices, such as the livery of crimson lake for passenger locomotives and rolling stock. Perhaps most notable was the continuation of the Midland Railway's small engine policy.

The arrival of the new Chief Mechanical Engineer, William Stanier, who had been head-hunted from the Great Western Railway by Josiah Stamp in 1933, heralded a change in the LMS. Stanier introduced new ideas, rather than continuing with the company's internal conflict.

The LMS, along with the other Big Three companies, was nationalized in 1948.

Stanier 8F

When Sir William Stanier took over as Chief Mechanical Engineer of the LMS, his most urgent priority was for mainline express and mixed traffic power. Prior to his appointment, the 'Midlandization' of the LMS was progressing with the construction of Midland-designed Compounds, 2P 4-4-0s and 4F 0-6-0s. Unfortunately, the philosophy of lots of small engines hauling lots of light trains was not suitable for the other areas of the LMS, particularly on the London and North Western section, with its tradition of large loads. As a result, there was a shortage of modern heavy freight power.

The preserved Great Central Railway, which runs between Loughborough and Leicester North stations, is one of the few places in the world where scheduled full-size steam trains can pass each other on double tracks. 48305 is seen waiting for its passengers at Loughborough station (above) and departing on a special evening charter (right).

SPECIFICATIONS

Class:	8F
Year:	1943
Wheel arrangement:	2-8-0
Cylinders:	2: 18½ x 28 inch
Driving wheel diameter:	4 x 8½ inch
Tractive effort:	32,438 lbs
Boiler pressure:	225 lbs
Valve gear:	Walschaerts
Coal capacity:	9 tons
Water capacity:	4,000 gallons

Recreating a scene from the heady days of steam, this is Loughborough station, which is kept beautifully clean and tidy. Colourful hanging baskets full of summer flowers greet the passengers.

The 8Fs started to make their appearance in 1937, and most were concentrated on the Midland lines, where something with considerable power was urgently required. As a Stanier locomotive they soon became popular, and the type was multiplied steadily up to the outbreak of war in 1939, by which time some 120 were running.

The type was chosen by the Ministry of Supply as the standard 'War' locomotive and construction was continued at the LMS works. In addition, large orders were placed with the North British

The cab of locomotive 48305, shows the gauges and levers that make the train drive. The red lever in the middle is known as the regulator and adjusts the flow of steam to the cylinders.

Many of this class were built for the War Department during World War Two. A large number never returned from war work, either being written off or being taken into stock on a Middle Eastern Railway.

Locomotive Co., with these latter locomotives being numbered in a separate War Department series. Many were shipped to the Middle East.

During the War, the locomotives were being produced at Swindon, Doncaster, Darlington and Brighton, in addition to the LMS works. The locomotives built at Doncaster were the first ever to be constructed there with Belpaire fireboxes. After the War, the 8Fs were concentrated in the London Midland Region and were augmented by some that were brought back from overseas. A few of the 8Fs survived to the end of steam in 1968.

Due to the heavy workload, this type of locomotive was designed for the eight driven wheels – one side of which can be seen on the right. These were fronted by two smaller, leading, non-driven carrying wheels (below).

Number 48305 was built in November 1943, and from 1950 it was working from the Wellingborough shed on the coal trains to Brent Sidings, Cricklewood and Toton. In April 1957, it was transferred to Northampton, and then to Crewe South in December 1962. It went to Northwich for three months before it made its final transfer to Speke junction in Liverpool, from where it was withdrawn in January 1968, arriving at Woodham's scrap yard at Barry in September of that year.

Restoration of 48305 was completed to British Railways unlined black livery in early 1995 and the engine returned to the Great Central Railway in April 2006. Towards the end of 2011, it was taken out of service for a ten-year overhaul.

Stanier Black 5

The LMS class 5 4-6-0, often referred to as the Black Five, was introduced by William Stanier in 1934, with a total of 842 examples being built. Many survived to the last day of steam with British Railways in 1968, and to date eighteen have been preserved. The Black 5 were a mixed traffic locomotive, and were seen to be very versatile. Numbering started from 5000, with the first twenty being ordered from Crewe Works, whilst a further eighty came from the Vulcan Foundry, who actually produced the first example, 5020, in 1934. The original engines were built with

Locomotive 45110 seen along the preserved Severn Valley Railway prior to crossing the viaduct that leads to Bewdley station.

domeless, straight throatplate boilers with low degree superheat (14 elements), however many received later-type boilers later in their lives. A further 227 were ordered from Armstrong-Whitworth in 1936 and Crewe built a further 142, which had domed, high degree superheat boilers. Number 5471, built at Crewe in 1938, was the last example to be built for five years due to the start of the Second World War.

Production was stopped during the War, but when it resumed in 1943 construction was restarted with Derby Works building its first example. In 1948 George Ivatt introduced further modifications to bearings and valve gear. Engine 4767 was built with Stephenson link motion in 1947, and 44738-57 were built with Caprotti valve gear. The last two, 44686 and 44687, built at Horwich in 1951, had even more modifications.

The numbering of the locomotives became slightly confused after the War too, with 5499 having to be the last in the run due to the next number being the start of the Patriot engines. The new numbers were started at 4800, but this was only good for a further 200 engines, when the numbers game had to start all over again. But, by this time, the LMS had been nationalized and was now under the British Rail banner, who added 4000 to all the numbers. So, eventually, the 842 examples were numbered 44658-45499.

44806 was built at Derby in 1944, being completed on July 15 that year. Preservation came in 1968, with the end of steam on

The evening shadows fall on locomotive 44806 as it builds power to haul its load of carriages out of Glyndyfrdwy station on the preserved Llangollen Railway.

British Rail. In July 2013, the locomotive was purchased by the North Yorkshire Moors Railway.

45110 was built in 1935 by the Vulcan Foundry. It was one of three members of the class to haul the 'Fifteen Guinea Special', Britain's last steam-hauled passenger train, on August 11, 1968. It was then preserved, and was put on display at Bridgnorth in 2013.

SPECIFICATIONS

Class:	5MT
Year:	1934 onwards
Wheel arrangement:	4-6-0
Cylinders:	2: 18½ x 28 inch
Driving wheel diameter:	6 ft
Tractive Effort:	25,450 lbs
Boiler pressure:	225 lbs
Valve gear:	Walschaerts
Coal capacity:	9 tons
Water capacity:	4,000 gallons

Fowler 7F

Locomotive 88, built by Robert Stevenson & Co. Ltd as part of the second batch in 1925, is seen making its way to Minehead Railway station.

The 7F 2-8-0 locomotive of the Somerset and Dorset Joint Railway (S&DJR), is a class of locomotive designed for heavy freight, and over the build period eleven were produced, in two batches, during 1914 and 1925.

At the time, the S&DJR was jointly owned by the Midlands Railway and the LSWR, who were in charge of the locomotive policy on the line. The lines here included some steep gradients, and the small engines of the Midlands Railway were not completely suitable, and so S&DJR locomotive superintendent M. H. Ryan pointed out that any future locomotive for this line should be specifically tailored to suit those conditions.

SPECIFICATIONS

Class:	7F
Year:	1925
Wheel arrangement	2-8-0
Cylinders:	2: 21 x 28 inch
Driving wheel diameter:	4 x 7½ inch
Tractive effort:	35,296 lbs
Boiler pressure:	190 lbs
Valve gear:	Walschaerts
Coal capacity:	4 tons
Water capacity:	3,500 gallons

The task of design was given to a draughtsman at Derby by the name of James Clayton, who came up with an exceptional piece of work that was unlike anything that had previously been seen at Derby. He combined the G9AS boiler of the Midland Compounds, with a Belpaire firebox and Walschaerts gear system, and with the addition of a leading truck, to help distribute the weight, the 2-8-0 configuration was complete.

The second batch of locomotives had larger boilers than the first, and were slightly shorter yet 2 tons heavier, giving a greater factor of adhesion.

The first batch of engines had right-hand driving positions, whereas the second batch were driven from the left. The cab of 88 shows its original number, which was later changed to 53808.

A double header is always an amazing sight to see. Here 53809 is heading a Raven class Q6, 63395, through Grosmont station in the Yorkshire Moors.

Cylinders were mounted high on the frame, and sloped to ensure no fouling of the platforms, and keeping in mind the gradients involved, two steam brake cylinders were provided for the engine and a further one for the tender.

Six of these locomotives were built in 1914, numbered 80-85 by the S&DJR, with a further five ordered in 1925 from Robert Stephenson and Hawthorns in Doncaster, equipped with the larger G9BS boiler and numbered 86-90.

All eleven locomotives constructed were based at Bath Green Park shed and were also withdrawn from there. The two featured here are the only ones that are preserved.

After being taken into LMS stock in 1928 and subsequently having their numbers changed to 13800-10, on nationalization British Railways added an extra 40000 to the numbers, thus they became 53800-10.

At the end of steam, 53808 and 53809 were sold to the Barry scrap yard. In 1968, the members of the S&D Railway Circle Trust rescued 53808, and 53809 was purchased privately in 1975. 53809 is preserved by the 13809 Locomotive Group, based at Butterley.

Ivatt Class 2MT

The LMS Ivatt Class 2 2-6-2T is a light, mixed traffic steam locomotive, introduced between 1946 and 1952. Although the LMS had various tank engines, by now they were getting quite old and something new was needed to replace them. George

Ivatt, noticing how successful the GWR 'Prairie' was, incorporated self-emptying ashpans and rocking grates into his new engine type.

Although the the first ten were built by the LMS (numbers 1200-9), the remaining 120 (41210-329) were built by British Rail

Built in 1951 at the Crewe works, 41312 is one of only three of this type to be rescued from the scrap yard. It is seen here on the Mid-Hants Railway, often referred to as the Watercress line.

SPECIFICATIONS

Class:	2MT
Year:	1946
Wheel arrangement:	2-6-2T
Cylinders:	2: 16 x 24 inch
Driving wheel diameter:	5 ft.
Tractive Effort:	17410 lbs
Boiler pressure:	200 lbs
Valve gear:	Walschaerts
Coal capacity:	3 tons
Water capacity:	1,350 gallons

Construction of the class continued until 1952, when it was superseded by the very similar new Standard 84000 Class. Some of the locomotives were fitted with a short but wide chimney, others with a tall narrow chimney, as in this case.

after nationalization in 1948 – BR having added the number '4' in front of the original numbers. Most of the engines were built at Crewe but the last ten came out of Derby. Fifty engines, 41210-20, 41270-89 and 41320-9 being fitted with push-pull equipment.

The last thirty engines to come from Crewe, 41290-41319, were earmarked for the Southern Region, whilst the rest became London Midland Region engines, all spending most of their working lives carrying out branch line duties. All engines were

Four of this class of locomotive have survived into preservation with 41241 being particularly associated with the Keighley and Worth Valley Railway. When it was initially preserved, it was painted in a fictitious maroon livery with K&WVR painted on the tanks, though it was later restored to more conventional BR black, as can be seen in these photographs.

withdrawn between 1962 and 1967, with four having survived into preservation.

41241 was built at Crewe in 1949 and worked from Bath Green Park and briefly at Highbridge on the Somerset & Dorset line. After a short spell at Leamington Spa, the engine went to Wellington, Shropshire in 1959. It was then sent to Bangor, Croes Newydd, Wrexham and Llandudno Junction for the Blaenau branch, ending up at Skipton in 1965. It was bought by the Keighley and Worth Valley Railway in 1967, and it hauled the train at the reopening of the branch line in 1968.

Feeling right at home with its long trail of goods wagons, 41241 builds up speed as it tackles the sloping exit to Keighley railway station.

41312 started service at Faversham, moving to Ashford in June 1959, before moving to Barnstaple Junction. Here she worked over the Torrington branch, appearing on occasions on the Ilfracombe and Exeter line. Her next stop was Brighton, before moving to Bournemouth in 1964, where she worked over the Swanage and Lymington branches. 41312 performed the last steam service on the Lymington branch in April 1967.

She saw the end of steam, and her final BR home was at Nine Elms. She was initially purchased from the Barry scrap yard by the Caerphilly Railway Society, but ended up at Ropley, Mid-Hants Railway for a major overhaul.

Fowler 4F

Taking a break from its duties on a busy steam weekend, 44422 awaits its turn to depart from Minehead railway station on the West Somerset Railway.

4422 was built at Derby Locomotive Works for the LMS Railway Company, to a design by Sir Henry Fowler. Originally developed for the Midland Railway Company, members of this class were designated as Superheater Freight Engines and carried a power classification of 4F. Produced between 1911 and 1927, 4422 was one of 772 examples manufactured. Its first allocation was to Leicester shed in 1927, with a subsequent transfer to Wigston in January 1929.

The engine moved to Bristol in 1940 and then Bath (Green Park) in 1948, spending the rest of its working life in south-west England. It worked on the Somerset and Dorset lines piloting West Country pacifics or Standard Class 9s across the Mendip Hills on holiday special duties.

British Railways acquired it after nationalization in 1948 and it was subsequently renumbered 44422. It was from Gloucester shed that 44422 was finally withdrawn from service in June 1965, where it then went to Woodham's scrap yard in South Wales. Here it languished for over eleven years before a team of preservationists from the North Staffordshire Railway Society raised the funds to buy it for restoration. The 4F was transferred by road to Cheddleton in April 1977 and the long haul to restoration began, with steaming taking place during September 1990.

Recently, 44422 has received a full overhaul and is back in traffic, currently on the East Lancashire Railway. Surviving the steam cull of the 1960s, this is one of four 4F engines in preservation, but is unique in being the sole left-hand drive example.

Midland Railway locomotives, of which the 4F took its design, were notorious for having problems with their short axle-box bearings, which were prone to overheating. It is confusing as to why the LMS 4F was allowed to inherit this fault.

SPECIFICATIONS

Class:	4F
Year:	1927
Wheel arrangement:	0-6-0
Cylinders:	2: 20 x 26 inch
Driving wheel diameter:	5 ft 3 inch
Tractive effort:	24,555 lbs
Boiler pressure:	175 lbs
Valve gear:	Stephenson
Coal capacity:	4 tons
Water capacity:	3,500 gallons

Fowler Class 3F

The LMS Fowler 3F 0-6-0T is often known as 'Jinty', and these steam engines represent the ultimate development of the Midland Railway's six-coupled tank engines. The design was based on rebuilds by Henry Fowler of the Midland Railway 2441 Class, introduced in 1899. They had a Belpaire firebox, wider side tanks, a larger bunker, an extended smokebox and a ventilator fitted in the roof of the cab.

They were built at the ex-L&YR Horwich Works, Bagnall's, Beardsmores, Hunslet, North British and the Vulcan Foundry, with a total of 422 being manufactured between 1924 and 1930. The first example built was originally numbered 13000, but the entire fleet was renumbered into the 7200 series in the 1932 renumbering exercise.

When the Second World War was declared in 1939, these engines were chosen by the War Department as their standard shunting locomotives; sadly the more modern Hunslet 'Austerity' 0-6-0ST was soon to replace it. All the same, they did see action when eight were despatched to France prior to its fall in 1940. Only five returned from France, of which two were sent to Ireland. Jinties could be seen at every shed and marshalling yard across the LMS network, being used for branch line and general freight work.

In 1948, nationalization saw the remaining 417 engines pass into British Railways' hands, with their new numbers being 47260-47681, although there were some gaps. Although many lasted to the end of steam, half had been withdrawn by 1964. Five lasted until 1967 and the last but one was withdrawn in 1967 – 47445 continued working with the National Coal Board.

47324 was built at the North British Locomotive Company in Hyde Park works in June 1926 as LMS 16407. She entered service at the former Caledonian Shed at Dawsholm, Glasgow, Scotland. In 1931 she was transferred to Ayr, where she was used as a station pilot. In August 1933 she was moved to Liverpool Edge Hill and then on to Liverpool Speke junction, where she was renumbered 7324 under the new scheme introduced by the LMS in early 1934.

Jinty 47324 moves cautiously with its wagons over the level crossing, while approaching Ramsbottom railway station on the preserved East Lancashire line.

Getting all steamed up and ready to push its wagons out of Keighley station is Jinty 47279. This type of engine was initially based in this area, and so they are a welcome and familiar sight.

SPECIFICATIONS

Class:	3F
Year:	1924
Wheel arrangement:	0-6-0T
Cylinders:	2: 18 x 26 inch
Driving wheel diameter:	4 ft 7 inch
Tractive effort:	20,835 lbs
Boiler pressure:	160 lbs
Valve gear:	Stephenson - side valves
Coal capacity:	2½ tons
Water capacity:	1,200 gallons

By 1939, she had moved across the Mersey to Birkenhead, where she remained for the next 27 years. In December 1966, 47324 (renumbered by BR) was withdrawn and made her last trip to Barry scrap yard. Although she was bought by the Fowler 3F society in 1978, more recently she could be seen regularly on the East Lancashire Railway.

47279 was one of the 422 built for the LMS and was used as a shunting, local goods and passenger engine – locomotives similar to this operated regularly on the Worth Valley branch in the 1930s. The engine returned to traffic on the Keighley and Worth Valley Railway in 1988. This ex-Barry scrap yard locomotive is now on its second stint of service, having returned to traffic after a quick but heavy overhaul in 2001.

Stanier Jubilee Class

Between 1934 and 1936, the LMS introduced 191 new 4-6-0 passenger locomotives, to work express trains on routes such as the former Midland line from St. Pancras. They were designed by Sir William Stanier and lasted into the 1960s, being withdrawn as a result of British Railways' modernization plans. In 1935, Jubilee 5642 exchanged identities with the first member of the class, 5552, and was specially turned out in a gloss black livery with all the brightwork, top feed cover, steam pipes and raised numbers

The setting sun exaggerates the steam coming from Leander as she slowly enters Rawtenstall station at the end of the East Lancashire Railway line.

chrome plated. The locomotive was named Silver Jubilee to commemorate the Silver Jubilee of King George V in 1935 – and so it was that they became the Jubilee Class.

It took a while for the locomotives to be given names, but when they did, 86 were given names from the British Empire: 39 admirals, 8 sea battles, 44 ships of the line, 8 early steam locomotives and the four provinces of Ireland. It was not until 1938 that the final locomotive was named.

The Jubilee Class locomotives were initially seen as a disappointment. Their moderate degree of superheating often left them short of steam, but changes to the blastpipe and chimney dimensions helped to transform them. Seen here is Leander at Ramsbottom.

SPECIFICATIONS

Class:	Jubilee
Year:	1936
Wheel arrangement:	4-6-0
Cylinders:	3: 17 x 26 inch
Driving wheel diameter:	6 ft 9 inch
Tractive effort:	26,610 lbs
Boiler pressure:	225 lbs
Valve gear:	Walschaerts
Coal capacity:	9 tons
Water capacity:	4,000 gallons

The Jubilees were given the classification of 5XP (BR 6P), and most of them retained this rating throughout their working lives. Two engines, however, were rebuilt with a larger boiler in 1942, and re-classified as 6P (BR 7P).

Initially, these engines were seen as unreliable, suffering from poor steaming problems, but as time went by these problems were

Although only built over a 3-year period, the class went through many improvements. For example, there were 10 boiler variations – mainly affecting the number of tubes. Early boilers were domeless, later ones domed. There were also 2 sizes of fire grate area, depending on whether the firebox throatplate was straight or sloping. Bogies also varied, as did the smokebox saddle, and a variety of tenders were fitted.

These locomotives are often associated with the Midland Division – the lines inherited from the former Midland Railway. This is due mainly to the fact that until the late 1950s it was rare to see any Class 7P (as it became) locomotives working south of Leeds.

resolved and they became hard-working engines, and could be found throughout the LMS area.

Even though these locomotives were a large class, they had a good safety record, with the most serious accident involving a Jubilee being the tragic crash at Harrow & Wealdstone in October 1952. This led to the withdrawal of 45637, Windward Islands, which was damaged beyond repair. Besides this engine, the first withdrawal was 45609, Gilbert and Ellice Islands, in September

1960. The last remaining locomotive, 45562, Alberta, was not withdrawn until November 1967, only a few months before steam on British Railways was completely ended.

Jubilee Class 5690 Leander was built at Crewe in March 1936 and named after HMS Leander, which, in turn, was named after the Greek hero Leander. After nationalization in 1948, she was renumbered 45690 by British Railways.

After being withdrawn in 1964, Leander was rescued from Woodham's scrap yard in Barry, South Wales, by the Leander Locomotive Society. Subsequently purchased by and run on the Severn Valley Railway, she was sold into private ownership and is now preserved at the East Lancashire Railway.

Ivatt Class 2MT

While William Stanier had concentrated on the introduction of larger engines, it was left to George Ivatt to design a new class of low-powered locomotive for the LMS line. What he came up with was a tender version of the Ivatt Class 2 2-6-2T, introduced at the same time, which was inspired by the Great Western 4500 and 4575 Classes. The 2-6-0s had a greater range due to their larger water and coal carrying capacity, making them well-suited to their task. Following some attention to draught problems by both Derby and Swindon works, they quickly became a success. The BR Standard Class 2 2-6-0

One of seven now in preservation, 46443 is seen at Kidderminster station on the Severn Valley Railway during a steam weekend.

SPECIFICATIONS

Class:	2MT
Year:	1946–1953
Wheel arrangement:	2-6-0
Cylinders:	2: 16 x 24 inches
Driving wheel diameter:	5 ft
Tractive effort:	17,410 lbs
Boiler pressure:	200 lbs
Valve gear:	Walschaerts
Coal capacity:	4 tons
Water capacity:	3,000 gallons

locomotives had BR standard fittings and a modified cab and tender profile. Both LMS and BR versions are often referred to by the nickname 'Mickey Mouse'.

A total of 128 were built between 1946 and 1953, mostly at Crewe. 20 were built by LMS (6400-19, becoming 46400-19 on nationalization in 1948). The remaining 108 (46420 to 46527) were built by British Railways. From 46465, an increase in cylinder diameter of half an inch yielded an increase of 1,100 lbs of tractive effort to 18,510 lbs. Thirty-eight (46465 to 46502) were built at Darlington, and were allocated to the Eastern and North Eastern regions, while the final 25 (46503 to 46527) were built at Swindon and allocated to the Western Region. The Swindon locomotives were turned out, initially, in lined black, although a few had lined green livery. The class was withdrawn between 1961 and 1967, and seven have been preserved.

The 2-6-0s, with their 3000-gallon water capacity and 4 tons of coal, had a long-range capability and were well suited to their task. Following attention to draughting problems, they quickly became a success.

Birth of the LNER

The London and North Eastern Railway was the second-largest of the 'Big Four' railway companies created by the Railways Act of 1921. It was created on January 1, 1923 and went through to nationalization in 1948. It was formed by the amalgamation of a number of constituent railway companies, of which the main ones were:

Great Eastern Railway

Great Central Railway

Great Northern Railway

Great North of Scotland Railway

Hull and Barnsley Railway

North British Railway

North Eastern Railway

The total route mileage was 6,590 (10,605 km) and the LNER now also owned 7,700 locomotives, 20,000 coaching vehicles, 29,700 freight vehicles, 140 pieces of electric rolling stock, six electric locomotives, ten rail motor cars, six turbine and 36 other steamers. It also owned a number of river boats and lake steamers, docks and harbours in 20 locations, some eastern Scottish ports, Harwich and London wharves, piers in similar places and 23 hotels. A few years later, in 1936, the Midland and Great Northern Joint Railway, the UK's largest joint railway, was also incorporated into the LNER.

The most common paint colours used by the LNER were lined apple green on its passenger locomotives and unlined black on freight locomotives, both with gold lettering.

Although the second-largest in terms of route miles, it was also the poorest of the 'Big Four'. It was famous for its prestigious high-speed trains, but also gained a lot of its income from the coal fields of north-east England. Routes varied from the flat agricultural lands of East Anglia to the severe curves and gradients of Scotland and the Pennines.

There were three Chief Mechanical Engineers of the LNER: Sir Nigel Gresley, Edward Thompson and Arthur H. Peppercorn.

Gresley A4

The A4 locomotives are probably the most famous of all the LNER Express Pacific designs. Distinctive in their streamlined styling, they symbolize 1930s luxury, elegance and fascination with speed.

The 1920s had seen an increase in competition for the railways, with more people travelling by car and airplane. By the 1930s, it

Shown here is the plaque carried by the Sir Nigel Gresley that confirms it is the holder of the post-war steam record speed of 112mph, gained on the 23 May 1959.

The crowds gather and look on as 60007 takes on water and coal. It's interesting to see the locomotive with the front streamlining panel open, revealing the original front-end.

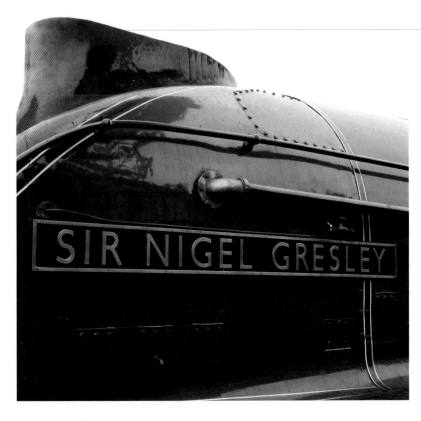

60007 was the 100th Gresley Pacific built and, as with the earlier LNER A4 Pacifics, was equipped with just the single chimney. It was fitted with a double chimney and Kylchap double blastpipe on December 13, 1957.

Several jets of steam and the shrill sound of the station master's whistle tells everybody that 60007 is ready to depart from the station at Grosmont, in the North Yorkshire countryside.

was obvious that travelling between major cities had to be faster, more reliable and more comfortable. German State Railways had produced the Fliegende Hamburger (Flying Hamburger), a diesel-electric, streamlined locomotive, and in 1934 the US Burlington Pioneer Zephyr, also streamlined and using a diesel engine, reached a speed of 112.5 mph (180 kph). Sir Nigel Gresley had seen both locomotives, travelled on the Flying Hamburger and was impressed with their streamlining.

Work was carried out on the A3s to make them go faster, the results of which were so well received that the LNER board gave Gresley the go-ahead to create what would become the 'Silver Jubilee' streamlined locomotives. The new A4 locomotives were introduced in 1935 to haul a new train called the 'Silver Jubilee' between London King's Cross and Newcastle, with the new service being named in celebration of the 25th year of King George V's reign.

The 'Silver Jubilee' was designed as a completely strealined locomotive, which included streamlined coaches too. Initially four were built, all having the word 'Silver' as part of their names, and during a press run to publicize the service, 'Silver Link' achieved a speed of 112.5 mph (180 kph), breaking the British speed record.

The first service was run on October 1, 1935, hauled by No. 2509 'Silver Link'. A further three locomotives were built for the Silver Jubilee service to Newcastle, which became a great success. This success led to an extension of the service to Edinburgh, and the building of a further five A4s. By 1937, a third service had

The Sir Nigel Gresley waits patiently for passengers to mount and dismount from the carriages. Following a 10-year overhaul, it was based at the North Yorkshire Moors railway for 2007.

With the beautiful backdrop of the North Yorkshire Moors, 60007 turns down the power as it approaches Levisham station, where it will wait for the upcoming train to pass in the station.

SPECIFICATIONS

Class:	A4
Year:	1935
Wheel arrangement:	4-6-2
Cylinders:	3: 18½ x 26 inches
Driving wheel diameter:	6 ft 8 inches
Tractive effort:	35,455 lbs
Boiler pressure:	250 lbs
Valve gear:	Walschaerts
Coal capacity:	8 tons
Water capacity:	5,000 gallon

commenced, and thus Britain's first inter-city network of fast train services was born.

So successful and reliable were these locomotives that extra coaches were added, bringing the total to eight. In the four years leading up to the Second World War, no A4 was ever involved in any major mishap, giving it a great safety record too.

As speeds slowly crept upwards, there were concerns about the ability for these huge machines to brake sufficiently well, and so a team from Westinghouse – the braking system chosen by Gresley – was commissioned to attend trials in 1938. The four-month-old A4 Mallard was the locomotive that was to be used for the trials, but little did the Westinghouse people know that this was going to be a particularly special occasion. Mallard was the first of the class to be fitted with the Kylchap double-blast pipe, and the designated driver

60019, named Bittern, was introduced on December 18, 1937, and was the last of the series to be withdrawn on September 5, 1966 from Aberdeen Ferryhill shed in Scotland.

Many of the Gresley A4s were named after birds, as in the case of Bittern. Initially based at Heaton in Newcastle, Bittern served the famous Flying Scotsman train between King's Cross and Newcastle.

had been changed. J. Duddington, well known for his ability to run trains hard when required, was chosen, along with fireman T. Bray and inspector J. Jenkins. Conventional brake tests were carried out on the down journey, but at Barkston, the Westinghouse team were given the choice of taking a taxi to Peterborough – it seems that they all refused!

The record attempt was described in this way:

'The centre big bearing was drowned in cylinder oil, and the return journey commenced. Grantham was passed at 24 mph (38.4 kph). By Stoke signal box, the speed had reached 74.5 mph (119.2 kph) with full regulator and 40 per cent cut-off. At milepost 94, 116 mph (185.6 kph) was recorded along with the maximum drawbar of 1800 hp. One hundred and twenty mph (192 kph) was achieved between milepost 92.75 and 89.75, and for a short distance of 306 yards, 125 mph (200 kph) was touched.'

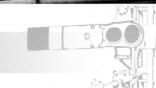

Originally numbered 4488, this A4 was named after the then newly formed Union of South Africa. On October 24, 1964 it pulled the last booked steam-hauled train from King's Cross, and was withdrawn from service in 1966.

There is some dispute over the top speed being 126 mph (201.6 kph), and Gresley himself refused to acknowledge that speed. And so, Mallard broke the world record for steam traction held by the German State Railways (124.5 mph/200.6 kph) and the British record set by the LMS (114 mph/182.4 kph). Over 60 years later, Mallard's record of 125 mph still stood.

The A4s did their bit for the war effort during World War Two, but after the hostilities it was the diesel engine that finally threatened their demise. However, due to the unreliability of the early diesels, the A4s continued longer than anticipated, with the first one being scrapped in 1962. The last British Rail A4 service was on September 14, 1966, between Aberdeen and Glasgow in Scotland.

The Great Marquess K4

The LNER Class K4 locomotive was designed specifically to cope with the unique steep gradients and severe curves of the then North British Railways West Highland line, which ran to Mallaig via Fort William in Scotland. Before 1923, the passenger services on this line were pulled by D34 'Glen' 4-4-0s, occasionally assisted by double headers. Solutions and proposals to the difficulties were debated, but in 1924 the Great Northern sent

The Great Marquess picks up speed as it crosses the Yorkshire Moors with its complement of carriages. The K4s were initially used on the Glasgow to Fort William stretch of the Scottish West Highland line.

fourteen K2s to the rescue, which remedied the situation, for a while at least.

In 1934, Sir Nigel Gresley instigated an investigation into the possibility of increasing the tractive effort of the K2s, and the next few years were spent drawing up solutions, based on a 1924 proposal for a 2-6-0 with 5 ft 2 inch coupled wheels, K3 cylinders, K2 boiler and B17 firebox, amongst other changes.

What came out was the new K4, the first of which was 3441 Loch Long, which went into service on January 28, 1937. The

SPECIFICATIONS

Class:	K4
Year:	1937
Wheel arrangement:	2-6-0
Cylinders:	3: 18½ x 26 inch
Driving wheel diameter:	5 ft 2 inches
Tractive effort:	36,598 lbs
Boiler pressure:	200 lbs
Valve gear:	Walschaerts
Coal capacity:	5 tons 10 cwt
Water capacity:	3,500 gallons

Note: Before June 1937, the boiler pressure was 180 lbs, and the tractive effort was 32,939 lbs.

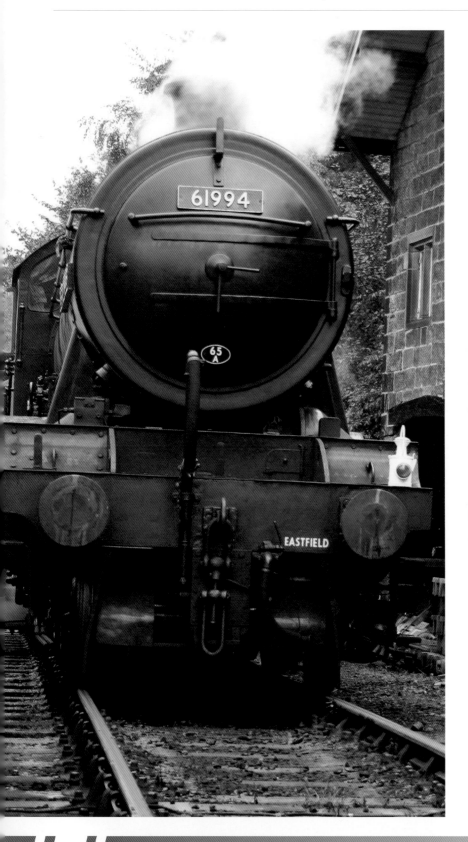

locomotives soon showed that they were more than capable of pulling the 300 ton load, and after an increase in boiler pressure a further five were ordered, which were put into service between 1938 and 1939. These would be the only K4s to be built, due to their specific requirements.

One of the six-strong K4 class locomotives made it into preservation. Bought from British Railways after withdrawal in 1961, 61994 The Great Marquess now runs regular rail tours as well as visiting many of the preserved lines.

Although the K4s handled the steep slopes and long curves well, they had a vibration problem on the long straight stretches of the line. This was rectified when they were replaced on the Glasgow to Fort William line by the Thompson B1s in 1947, with the new Thompson/Peppercorn K1s appearing just two years later.

After nationalization, the K4s were assembled at Eastfield and intended for use on West Highland goods trains only. In 1959, all were concentrated at Thornton Junction depot in Fife, but were withdrawn in October 1961. The last K4, 61994 The Grand Marquess, was saved by Viscount Garnock and is now in preservation.

The K4s were popular with the crews, but a vibration over long, fast stretches caused maintenance problems and an uncomfortable ride.

The Q6 was an unglamorous freight workhorse seen on the tracks of the north-east of England. Seen here is one of the last survivors, 63395, recapturing the last heady days of steam.

Raven Q6

Although the Q5 0-8-0s of William Wordsall had helped to meet the increase in Northern Railways' mineral traffic, the continual rise in traffic requirements, and that of more power, was still there at the start of the 20th century. Vincent Raven continued the good work and designed his Q6 class locomotive to help ease the situation further. One hundred and twenty of this class were built at Darlington Works between 1913 and 1921. He used the best parts of the piston valve version of the Q5 design, along with a larger boiler and a saddle fitting for the smokebox. Having also fitted superheaters to many of the B15 4-6-0s, he was convinced that the Q6s should also have them, which they were then given as standard. With this combination, Raven had produced a strong and reliable locomotive that would give good service and last through to the end of the steam era. Few modifications were made during its lifespan – Robinson superheaters replaced the original Schmidt version, although this was more to keep in line with current LNER practice than anything else.

The Q6s had no train-braking ability, apart from one brake cylinder that operated the brake on the tender and the locomotive, which meant that they could not pull passenger trains, unless in exceptional circumstances.

These dependable engines were initially allocated to sheds in the north-east, but occasionally they would be used for medium- and long-distance freight, as well as the heavy mineral traffic for which they were designed. As the diesel engine started to take a grip, so the Q6s were replaced, with general withdrawals starting in 1963, and the last Q6 being withdrawn in 1967.

Locomotive 2238 (3395 in the 1946 scheme, and BR 63395) has survived into preservation and can often be seen operating on the North Yorkshire Moors Railway (NYMR). 2238 re-entered traffic in 2007 after a major overhaul.

Due to commitments with other NELPG (the North Eastern Locomotive Preservation Group) locomotives, 63395 had to take a back seat. As pressure grew for its return to steam, 2000 saw a start on its major overhaul. It was the most comprehensive in the NELPG's history, with completion in 2007.

SPECIFICATIONS

Class:	Q6
Year:	1913
Wheel arrangement:	0-8-0
Cylinders:	2: 20 x 26 inch
Driving wheel diameter:	4 ft 7½ inches
Tractive effort:	28,800 lbs
Boiler pressure:	180 lbs
Valve gear:	Stephenson
Coal capacity:	5½ tons
Water capacity:	4,125 gallons

Peppercorn K1

The 62005 was designed by the LNER and built by the North British Locomotive Company at their Queen's Park Works, Glasgow. It was delivered to British Railways in June 1949. Although the design is attributed to A. H. Peppercorn, its history

The Jacobite run from Fort William, Scotland, covers some spectacular scenery, but probably the most famous part of the journey is when the train crosses the Glenfinnan Viaduct. This mighty 21-arched, 1200-foot bridge, constructed in 1901, was the first concrete-built viaduct in the world.

goes back to the Great Northern Railway (GNR), when a certain Sir Nigel Gresley was CME. His first design, very much influenced by the North American 2-6-0 wheel configuration, became the GNR class H2, later to become the original LNER class K1, which finally developed into the K4s. Following Gresley's death in 1941, Edward Thompson took over the post of CME and made modifications to prototype K4 3445 MacCailin Mor. These proved to be successful, and were added to when A. H. Peppercorn replaced Thompson after

The first outline drawing for a two-cylinder rebuild of a K4 appeared in February 1945. 3445 MacCailin Mor was chosen as the guinea pig for the new class. Modifications included replacing the original double swing link pony truck with a spring side control pony truck, the cylinders were of a standard Thompson design as used on his B1 4-6-0s, and the original K4 cab was retained, although the sides were altered to fit the new running plate. On becoming CME, Peppercorn used this rebuild as the basis of his new K1 Class.

*The beautiful Scottish countryside is an ideal background for
62005 as she makes her way to Mallaig from Fort William (above).
Spoked 5 ft 2 inch coupled wheels, including counterweights,
and Walschaerts gear drives can be seen on 62005 (left). A larger,
longer tender was also included with the new K1, which carried
4200 gallons of water rather than the K4s 3500 gallons (right).*

his retirement. With this, a batch of 70 was ordered from the North
British Locomotive Company, which was delivered to the newly
formed British Railways in 1949. All the original LNER K1s had been
converted to K2s by 1937, and so this new locomotive acquired the
K1 classification, with the prototype being known as K1/1.

SPECIFICATIONS

Class:	K1
Year:	1949
Wheel arrangement:	2-6-0
Cylinders:	2: 20 x 26 inch
Driving wheel diameter:	5 ft 2 inches
Tractive effort:	32,081 lbs
Boiler pressure:	225 lbs
Valve gear:	Walschaerts
Coal capacity:	7 tons 10 cwt
Water capacity:	4,200 gallons

Originally based at New England, K1/1 took over the operations usually run by K2s and K3s. Following a number of allocations to the Edinburgh and New England areas, it moved to Fort William in 1954, where it remained until its withdrawal in June 1961.

After being condemned in 1967, 62005 was sold to a consortium in 1969, with a view to saving its boiler for K4 61994, The Great Marquess. Up to that point it had been used for a brief period as a temporary stationary boiler on the ICI North Tees Works. The boiler was eventually kept intact and the locomotive was donated to the NELPG in 1972 and delivered to the British Rail Thornaby Depot in June of that year.

More recently, 62005 could be seen working the Fort William to Mallaig Jacobite run in Scotland.

Riddles Austerity Class

Robert Arthur Riddles was appointed Director of Transport Equipment at the Ministry of Supply at the start of World War Two. By 1941 he had been appointed Deputy Director-General of Royal Engineer Equipment, and by the following year had started his designs for a new 'Austerity' 2-8-0.

Double heading its way out of Keighley station is the train that never was. Shipped to the continent and sold to the Netherlands State Railways, it became their 4300 class number 4464. Only after returning and being completely restored did it become 90733.

Based on the Stanier 8F, the current chosen military goods locomotive, construction started in January 1943, and a total of 935 locomotives were built by May 1945, by the North British Locomotive Co. and Vulcan Works. Keeping in mind the great lack of materials during the war years, these locomotives were basic and generally quite crude. With many parts interchangeable with the 8F, a simpler parallel boiler with round-topped firebox design was used, which did cause some problems. The 'Austerities' were fitted with steam brakes and Westinghouse air brake equipment, but between 1946 and 1948 the LNER removed the air pumps.

Before the Normandy landings, the Army had very little use for these locomotives, so they were lent to the 'Big Four' railways; of 457 locomotives, the LNER received 350. After June 1944, 'Austerity' locomotives were shipped out to France, and by February 1945 all were transferred to the Continent.

At the end of 1946, the LNER purchased 200 'Austerities', including 190 that it already had on loan, and with the war over and ownership now permanent, they became classified as Class O7 in January 1947. These locomotives were also designed for easy conversion to oil firing, and due to the post-war fuel crisis this was attempted, but with little satisfaction. On January 26, 1949, British Railways dropped the 'O7' classification and they became simply 'WD 2-8-0s', while also gaining the nickname of 'Bed Irons' due to the loud clanking noises produced by their motion.

Scheduled withdrawals started in earnest in 1962, and the last five WD 2-8-0s were withdrawn in September 1967.

Parading as the Thames Clyde Express, 90733 is seen approaching Oxenhope station, the southern terminus of the Keighley and Worth Valley Railway.

SPECIFICATIONS

Class:	Austerity
Year:	1943
Wheel arrangement:	2-8-0
Cylinders:	2: 19 x 28 inch
Driving wheel diameter:	4 ft 8½ inches
Tractive effort:	34,215 lbs
Boiler pressure:	225 lbs
Valve gear:	Walschaerts
Coal capacity:	9 tons
Water capacity:	5,000 gallons

No LNER 07 survived into preservation. However, WD 2-8-0, Works No. 5200, built by the Vulcan Foundry in 1945 and sent to Europe, where it joined the Swedish strategic reserve, is now preserved and running. Heavily modified in Sweden, it was purchased by a group of volunteers at the Keighley & Worth Valley Railway and operated services until 1976. Restored back to its original condition with a rebuilt tender and new cab, and renumbered 90733 – continuing the sequence of BR numbered 2-8-0 'Austerity' locomotives – it returned to traffic in the summer of 2007.

Gresley V2 Green Arrow

One of Sir Nigel Gresley's most successful designs, the V2 became the LNER's best known mixed traffic locomotive type. A total of 184 were built in eleven batches, between 1936 and 1944 at the Doncaster and Darlington works, with the final locomotive, number 3695, being delivered in July 1944. Four more were planned in the last batch, but Thompson had these built to his A2/1 Pacific design.

4771 Green Arrow was built in June 1936 for the LNER at Doncaster, and was given that name in connection with the freight

Green Arrow picks up speed after leaving Bewdley station. The Seven Valley Railway suffered badly from the floods in 2007 and only the Kidderminster to Bewdley section of the preserved line was open for use.

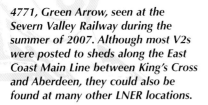

4771, Green Arrow, seen at the Severn Valley Railway during the summer of 2007. Although most V2s were posted to sheds along the East Coast Main Line between King's Cross and Aberdeen, they could also be found at many other LNER locations.

line it served. It was the first to be built in its class, and was designed for hauling express freight and passenger trains.

When World War Two started, production of the V2s did not stop, unlike many of the other locomotives. They had proved to be incredible work-horses and their pulling power was superior to most – on more than one occasion a single V2 hauled 26 coaches from Peterborough to London. Production finally did stop in 1944, and they became the last Gresley designs to be produced.

Shortly after World War Two, there was a spate of V2 accidents which involved derailment and excessive speed; a contributing

SPECIFICATIONS

Class:	V2
Year:	1936
Wheel arrangement:	2-6-2
Cylinders:	3: 18½ x 26 inch
Driving wheel diameter:	6 ft 2 inches
Tractive effort:	33,730 lbs
Boiler pressure:	220 lbs
Valve gear:	Walschaerts
Coal capacity:	7 tons 10 cwt
Water capacity:	4,200 gallons

An early morning start for loco 4771, as she steams up just outside Toddington Railway Station on the Gloucestershire Warwickshire Railway (GWR).

Initial designs for the V2 incorporated streamlining, which was eventually done away with, although the partially streamlined cab was kept.

factor also being the deterioration of the track. Maintenance of the railway infrastructure during the war had been poor and the whole railway system had been somewhat neglected. One of the problems was also thought to be the Gresley double swing link pony truck design, which may have been very sensitive to the poor condition of the tracks. Modifications were carried out, with all V2s benefiting in 1947, after which, along with track improvements, there was only one further V2 derailment, in 1952.

The 1960s saw trials being carried out with Kylchap blastpipe/chimney arrangements, but no significant power boost was noted. Further trials were then carried out with Kylchap cowls,

Green Arrow turns on the power as she pulls away from Winchcombe station, which is actually at Greet, in the beautiful Cotswold countryside.

which resulted in a significant increase in performance, comparable to that of the Pacifics. It was decided to modify all V2s, but with the coming of the diesel locomotive, only eight were actually changed to the double chimney Kylchap arrangement.

Withdrawal of these locomotives started in February 1962, with the last V2 being withdrawn on December 6, 1966 – this was also the last of Gresley's big engines to be withdrawn.

The pioneer V2, 60800 (LNER 4771) Green Arrow, was withdrawn in August 1962, and is the only one in preservation. Once withdrawn, it was due to go to the new Leicester Municipal Museum, after being restored at Doncaster. This didn't happen, but it was taken in by the National Collection at York and later restored to running condition. Since then, Green Arrow has been seen regularly on many BR tracks and has become a favourite with enthusiasts and the general public alike.

A rare treat for any enthusiast. An early morning scene shows two well-known locomotives side by side. On the left is Green Arrow, and with her front just jutting out from behind on the right is 3440 City of Truro.

Gresley D49

By 1925, Gresley had completed his work to build up numbers of the A1 Pacifics, and so now he concentrated all his efforts on a design for an intermediate express locomotive. The new engine would have to be powerful for its size, and so his three-cylinder arrangement with patented conjunctive valve gear layout was chosen, along with a 4-4-0 wheel arrangement.

The design was completed at the beginning of 1926, and the first example, 234 Yorkshire, was completed at Darlington the following year.

A total of 76 were built in three main examples between 1927 and 1935. Twenty-eight D49/1s with conventional piston valves were built in three batches between 1927 and 1929. Forty-two D49/2s with rotary cam-operated Lentz poppet valves were built between 1929 and 1935. Only six D49/3s, which also used rotary

D49 Locomotive 246 Morayshire was overhauled in early 2000, and by 2003 she was making regular journeys on the Bo'ness & Kinneil Railway. She is seen here travelling along the coastal route out of Bo'ness.

cam-operated Lentz poppet valves, were built in 1928. These were all rebuilt as D49/1s in 1938; the D49/1s were named after Shire counties, and the D49/2s were named after fox hunts – they would also become the last 4-4-0 design to be built by the LNER.

Most of the D49s were sent to the Scottish and North Eastern areas, many being allocated to St Margarets, Dundee and Eastfield, with a limited number sent to Perth and Haymarket. During the Second World War they were often found working as goods trains, and post-war they were used for stopping passenger services on main lines – due to their high axle-loading they were not suited to the branch lines.

When Edward Thompson became CME in 1941, he instigated a major standardization programme in which a class 'D' was planned. By 1942, 365 was chosen as the first rebuild to that class, but it never performed well, and by the time of nationalization any further rebuilds to class D were cancelled by British Rail. By now the D49s were being replaced by Thompson 4-6-0s and relegated to minor duties. The mid-1950s saw many being substituted by the new diesel multiple units, and just a couple of years later, in 1957, withdrawal started.

The last withdrawal was 246 Morayshire, which was purchased privately and donated to the Royal Scottish Museum. It was restored to running condition but spent much of the 1980s and 1990s in static condition. Morayshire returned to running condition in 2005 and is now a regular on the Bo'ness & Kinneil Railway.

Last-minute preparations (below) are made on Morayshire before leaving Bo'ness station (right). Due to their draughty cabs and poor ride, these locomotives were not favoured by the Scottish crews of the period.

SPECIFICATIONS

Class:	D49
Year:	1927
Wheel arrangement:	4-4-0
Cylinders:	3: 17 x 26 inch
Driving wheel diameter:	6 ft 8 inches
Tractive effort:	21,556 lbs
Boiler pressure:	180 lbs
Valve gear:	Walschaerts
Coal capacity:	4 tons 10 cwt
Water capacity:	3,300 gallons

The above specifications are for the D49/1. D49/2, D49/3 and D (often referred to as D49/4) variations followed.

Thompson B1

With the sudden death of Sir Nigel Gresley in 1941, the position of CME at the LNER was given to Edward Thompson, who instigated a much-needed programme of standardization and modernization. With this he would create the most successful of his locomotive designs, the 4-6-0 Thompson B1.

The first engine diagrams were presented in November 1941, and closely resembled the classic Gresley look of the B17 'Sandringham' Class. By 1942 these had been simplified, with special attention being given to the cab, running plate and steam pipe casings. This all tied in with Thompson's thoughts on simplicity of design, maintenance and standardization, also keeping in mind the current wartime conditions. With further changes being applied, such as increasing the boiler pressure and introducing a significant new bogie design, the construction of the B1s started in mid-1942.

The first in this class, 8301 Springbok, named in honour of a visit by General Smuts – prominent South African and British Commonwealth statesman – was presented in the same year. Naming of the B1s followed this train of thought and became the 'Antelope' class, although some were also known as 'Bongoes'. The initial 41 B1s were given antelope names when built, while eighteen more were named after construction, and carried names of

Recreating a locomotive that once was, this is 61264 dressed as 61039 Steinbok, which was built at the LNER Darlington works in 1947 but eventually scrapped.

After being converted to a stationary boiler, 61264 avoided scrapping by becoming the only LNER locomotive to be withdrawn to the famous Barry scrap yard in South Wales. It is seen here heading through the Esk Valley towards Grosmont station.

SPECIFICATIONS

Class:	B1
Year:	1942
Wheel arrangement:	4-6-0
Cylinders:	2: 20 x 26 inch
Driving wheel diameter:	6 ft 2 inches
Tractive effort:	26,878 lbs
Boiler pressure:	225 lbs
Valve gear:	Walschaerts
Coal capacity:	7½ tons
Water capacity:	4,200 gallons

Note: The above details are for the original B1s.

LNER directors. Only one was named after nationalization, 61379 Mayflower, in 1951.

Although a total of 410 were manufactured, it is interesting to note that on March 7, 1950, locomotive 61057 crashed into a stationary goods train in dense fog. Beyond repair, it was scrapped and no replacement was ordered. Thus, only 409 remained in service, not the intended 410.

Although the B1 went through the upgrading process during its life, no major developments in the design were instigated, partly due to its original robustness, but also because of the impending emergence of the diesel locomotive.

Besides 61057's accident, the first B1 was withdrawn in November 1961, with the last three being withdrawn in September 1967. Many were converted for use as stationary boilers, but all were withdrawn by 1968.

Two Thompson B1s have survived into preservation, 61264, which has been preserved by the Thompson B1 Locomotive Trust and 61306, Mayflower, which is owned by the Mayflower Group. The original Mayflower was scrapped, and the name was transferred with the casting of new nameplates.

Gresley A1/A3 Flying Scotsman

The Flying Scotsman is probably the most famous steam locomotive in the world, and its number 4472 is recognized by enthusiasts and spotters from all over. It hasn't always carried that number, and in fact was originally built as an A1 locomotive and given the number 1472. Along with a new name, the number change came when, as an LNER flagship locomotive, it represented the company at the British Empire Exhibition at Wembley in 1924 and 1925.

In its original A1 guise, this locomotive was built in 1923 at the Doncaster Works from a design created by Sir Nigel Gresley. It was used as a long-distance express train, in particular on the Flying Scotsman service (from where the locomotive also acquired its name) between London King's Cross and Edinburgh in Scotland.

Looking truly at home, Flying Scotsman returns to its place of birth. Doncaster works, generally known as 'the Plant', was established by the Great Northern Railway in 1853 to replace the Boston and Peterborough works.

The National Railway Museum, based in York, purchased the Flying Scotsman in 2004, following which it had a complete overhaul before being put back into service.

On November 30, 1934, and running a light test train, 4472 became the first steam locomotive to be officially recorded at 100 mph (160 kph), thus stamping its mark in the history books with a place in the land speed records for railed vehicles.

The Flying Scotsman went through several designation changes – A3 after having received a boiler with a long 'banjo' dome of the type it carries today, and it became number 103 in Edward Thompson's comprehensive renumbering scheme, before advancing to 60103 during nationalization.

4472 ended its service with British Railways in 1963 and was sold for preservation when it was restored as closely as possible to its original LNER condition. It then worked a number of rail tours, including a non-stop London-Edinburgh run in 1968 – the year that steam traction officially ended on BR. In 1969 it went on a promotional tour to the USA, where it was fitted with a cowcatcher, high-intensity headlamp, bell, air brakes and buckeye couplings. Financial problems saw its owners bankrupted, and fears then arose for the engine's future. Fortunately, in January 1973 William McAlpine stepped in at the eleventh hour and had the locomotive repaired and repatriated.

In 1988 the locomotive travelled to Australia to take part in the country's bicentenary celebrations. There it set another record, travelling 442 miles from Parkes to Broken Hill non-stop, the longest such run by a steam locomotive ever recorded.

SPECIFICATIONS

Class:	A1/A3
Year:	1923
Wheel arrangement:	4-6-2
Cylinders:	3: 20 x 26 inches
Driving wheel diameter:	6 ft 8 inches
Tractive effort:	29,835 lbs
Boiler pressure:	180 lbs
Valve gear:	Walschaerts
Coal capacity:	8 tons
Water capacity:	5,000 gallons

In 1995 it was in pieces at Southall depot in West London and once again facing an uncertain future, owing to the cost of restoration and refurbishment necessary to meet the stringent engineering standards required for main-line operation. Salvation came a year later, when Dr Tony Marchington bought the locomotive and restored it to running condition. In 2004 The Flying Scotsman was put up for sale because of the mounting debts of its owning company, and it was bought by the National Railway Museum in York. It is now part of the national collection.

Birth of the Southern Railway

The Southern Railway existed between 1923 and 1948, and geographically was the smallest of the four companies to come out of the grouping ordered by the Railways Act of 1921.

The Southern Railway owned no track north of London, but in the south and south-east of the country it had a virtual monopoly, although in certain places in the south-west it was in competition with the Great Western Railway.

The major constituents of the Southern Railway were:

The London and South Western Railway (LSWR)

The London, Brighton and South Coast Railway (LBSCR)

The combined South Eastern Railway and London, Chatham and Dover Railway, under the South Eastern & Chatham Railways' Managing Committee (SECR)

The three Isle of Wight railways

Lynton and Barnstaple Railway

Several light railways, including the Basingstoke and Alton Light Railway; although other candidate lines remained independent, such as the Kent and East Sussex Railway

Tracks making up 2,186 route miles (3,518 km)

Other assets also included 2,390 locomotives, 10,800 coaching vehicles, 37,500 freight vehicles, 460 electric vehicles, 14 rail motor cars, 38 large turbines or other steamers, a number of other vessels and 3.5 miles of canals.

Also incorporated were docks, harbours and equipment at several south coast towns, ten large hotels, London termini, including Waterloo (the largest London railway station), Victoria, Charing Cross, Cannon Street and London Bridge (the oldest London terminus).

The Chief Mechanical Engineers (CME) of the Southern Railway, responsible for locomotives and rolling stock, were R. E. L. Maunsell from 1922 to 1937 and O. V. S. Bulleid, who remained until nationalization. Bulleid in particular is classed as an outstanding engineer, designing the Merchant Navy class, the West Country and Battle of Britain classes (Bulleid Light Pacifics), the Q1 and the experimental Leader, as well as a host of innovative electrical units and locomotives.

The company was left devastated after the war, and was nationalized in 1948, being incorporated into the newly formed single countrywide operation British Railways, but it largely survived as the Southern Region.

West Country and Battle of Britain

The Southern Railways' West Country and Battle of Britain classes were also known as Light Pacifics or 'Spam Cans'. Like the Merchant Navy Class, they too were fitted with 'air-smoothed' streamlining and many of the other innovative designs which Oliver Bulleid had incorporated into the Merchant Navy class of locomotive. One important novelty was the ability to use welding for the construction process, in preference to riveting, which meant that components could be made quicker and easier. This was beneficial during a period of wartime austerity and post-war economy.

In 1950, Battle of Britain Class steam locomotive 34081, seen here, was named 92 Squadron. She runs regularly through the Kent countryside to the delight of many enthusiasts.

SPECIFICATIONS

Class:	West Country/Battle of Britain (as built)
Year:	1945
Wheel arrangement:	4-6-2
Cylinders:	3: 16⅜ x 24 inches
Driving wheel diameter:	6 ft 2 inches
Tractive effort:	31,000 lbs
Boiler pressure:	250 lbs
Valve gear:	Bulleid chain-drive
Coal capacity:	5 tons
Water capacity:	4,500 gallons

When Southern Railways introduced the Merchant Navy Class, nobody had ever seen anything like them before, and they went on to become very successful. However, the new West Country and Battle of Britain classes needed to be much lighter than their sister locomotive, allowing them to be more versatile and able to cover more of their lesser-used lines. Bulleid therefore used the Merchant Navy Class locomotive as a template and designed a lighter and smaller locomotive that could be easily maintained. With its 4-6-2 wheel arrangement, generally giving better high-speed running, and a large firebox for increased boiler efficiency, these locomotives also became known as Bulleid Light Pacifics, in contrast to the heavier Merchant Navy Class. These lighter engines incorporated most of the innovative design features seen on the Merchant Navy Class locomotives, such as the Bulleid chain-drive valve gear, electric lighting and the Bulleid-Firth-Brown (BFB) wheel design. These smaller locomotives became a true mixed-traffic design, able to cope with both passenger and freight work, and thus being used on a variety of lines around the south of England. From the channel ports of the south-east to the seaside resorts of the West Country, these locomotives took their role of express, semi-fast passenger, and freight trains with pride.

Many of the preserved locomotives visit other lines besides their own. Here, for example, is 34081 seen on the Swanage Railway line just approaching Norden station.

It's easy to see why these beautifully streamlined locomotives attract so many enthusiasts. They are so different to the other locomotives, with their slick bodywork and front air-deflectors.

34081 '92 Squadron' is named after the famous Spitfire squadron based at Biggin Hill, Kent during the Battle of Britain in 1940.

The front ends of these locomotives were quite different to the Merchant Navy Class engines and were much more enclosed but, all the same, were viewed by many as a streamlining addition. This was not the view of Bulleid, though, who had intended the design to be an aid in cleaning the locomotive via the use of a carriage washer, another attempt to reduce labour requirements during the post-war period, while at the same time creating a unique locomotive. The tender too had streamlining panels, generally known as 'raves', which gave the top a similar cross-sectional look to the carriages the locomotive was pulling.

A total of 110 Light Pacific locomotives were built, of which seventy were constructed by Southern Railways at the Brighton works. The first West Country Class prototype, 21C101 Exeter, was completed in May of 1945, and the last, being Battle of Britain Class 21C170 Manston, was completed in November of 1947. A final batch of forty locomotives were constructed after nationalization in 1948, which had several differences to the original engines – obviously there was no Southern Railways number, the footplate was larger and the tender had an increased water-carrying capacity, to name a few. From the locomotives run by Southern Railways, 48 were named after seaside resorts in the West Country served by its

On steam weekends the Sussex countryside is alive with the sound of steam trains. Here, Wadebridge is making its way to Horsted Keynes station along the Bluebell Railway.

trains or close to its lines, and the rest took their names from Royal Air Force-related objects such as squadrons, airfields, commanders and aircraft which took part in the Battle of Britain over the county of Kent.

Much like their sister engines, the Light Pacifics also went through rebuild. During the late 1950s, British Rail modified sixty of the class, removing their streamlined casing and replacing it with conventional boiler cladding. The Bulleid chain-driven valve gear was also replaced with a modified Walschaerts valve gear system. These changes added to the overall weight of the locomotive, and resulted in the trains not being able to work on certain lines, something that they had been specifically designed for. With this

restriction and the onset of modernization plans during the early 1960s, the remaining fifty locomotives were never rebuilt, and continued in original specification until they were eventually withdrawn from service.

The classes operated until July 1967, when the last steam locomotives on the Southern Region were withdrawn from service, and although most were subsequently scrapped, twenty managed to escape the dreaded cutting torch. It is interesting to note that if it had not been for Woodham's scrap yard in South Wales, where these locomotives ended up, no rebuilt Light Pacifics would have

been preserved. Today, it is a real treat to see one of these wonderful locomotives steaming its way through the Sussex countryside, with visions of Spitfire aircraft fighting German fighter planes in the skies above.

The first Bulleid Light Pacifics appeared in 1945 and they would be used on the restricted secondary routes, where the heavier Merchant Navy Class locomotives were prohibited. The West of England was one particular region, which also prompted the SR to call them the West Country Class – this is Wadebridge.

A magnificent looking Blackmoor Vale stands at Sheffield Park station on the Bluebell Railway, awaiting that shrill sound from the station masters whistle that will let the driver know it's time to leave.

• 92 SQUADRON

In September 1948, Battle of Britain Class locomotive 34081 was released to traffic at Ramsgate shed and used on prestigious express lines such as the 'Thanet Belle', 'The Man of Kent', 'Night Ferry' and the 'Golden Arrow', along with other commuter trains.

In April 1950 she was repainted in Brunswick Green at Brighton works and had her nameplates affixed for the first time – 92 Squadron. Following the Kent electrification scheme, she was sent to Exmouth Junction shed, in September 1957. Here she was used on services to North Devon and Cornwall, including the famous 'Atlantic Coast Express', as well as to London. A brief visit to Eastleigh shed then saw her withdrawn from service and sent to Barry scrap yard in South Wales.

On 5 November 1976, 34081 departed Barry scrap yard by low-loader, and thus became the 86th engine to escape the cutting torch into preservation.

• WADEBRIDGE

The oldest surviving West Country Class locomotive was built at Brighton in 1945, leaving the works in August as 21C107 and venturing west to Wadebridge for her official naming ceremony on 31 October of that year.

Allocated from new to Exmouth Junction shed, her early years were spent in the West Country, until 11 April, 1951, when she moved to Nine Elms, the shed for Waterloo, London. She was re-painted in standard BR Brunswick Green and her cab modified to wedge-shaped. She operated mainly on the old LSWR tracks to Bournemouth, Weymouth and Salisbury, frequently to be seen on Ocean Liner special trains, and was even known to have worked 'The Royal Wessex'.

On 14 September 1964 she was transferred to Salisbury shed for her final few months, but on 7 October 1965 she was sold to Woodham's scrap yard in South Wales, having escaped a BR rebuild. She languished in the yard until 1981, at which time she was purchased for preservation.

• BLACKMOOR VALE

The West Country Class locomotive was completed at Brighton in February 1946, receiving the name 'Blackmoor Vale' in August 1947. It was renumbered 34023 in April 1948, and then repainted in April 1950, at which time it received 'Blackmore Vale' nameplates, which it retained apart from a short spell in 1963 when it carried, on one side only, an unofficial O. V. Bulleid nameplate. In preservation, the 1950 nameplates have been removed for safe-keeping, and the locomotive has carried replica plates as 'Blackmoor Vale', correct for the Southern malachite green livery. Blackmoor Vale came to the Bluebell Railway via initial preservation at Longmoor,

In 1956 a scheme by British Railways to rebuild some 60 of the class to a more conventional design resulted in Bodmin – featured here – losing its air-smoothed casing (streamlining), along with other modifications.

Blackmoor Vale in full motion across the Sussex countryside on its way to Horsted Keynes station. Many of the West Country locomotives sported an additional plaque depicting the coat of arms associated with the town or region the locomotive was named after. This plaque was mounted on the casing between the locomotive nameplate and the West Country Class scroll, above the middle driving wheel.

having been one of the last Bulleid Pacifics running on British Rail. Unlike many of its classmates it was not rebuilt, retaining Bulleid's 'air-smoothed' casing and oil-bath-enclosed valve gear.

• BODMIN

34016 was named after a town in Cornwall and is, therefore, a West Country Class Pacific locomotive. Bodmin was completed in November 1945, given the number 21C116 and named by the Mayor of Bodmin on 28 August, 1946. In 1948, Bodmin was re-numbered 34016 by British Railways following nationalization, and worked in the Devon area until 1958.

In 1956, a scheme by British Railways to rebuild some 60 of the class to a more conventional design resulted in Bodmin losing some of her original features. She then worked in Kent before being based at Eastleigh for her final years in service. She was withdrawn in June 1964 and sent to Barry scrap yard in South Wales in February 1965.

Bodmin was rescued in 1971 and re-entered service after restoration on 8 September 1979.

• EDDYSTONE

West Country Class 21C128 Eddystone was built at Brighton works in April 1946, and went straight into traffic from Ramsgate, where it took up regular duties on the Kent Coast services to Victoria and Cannon Street, London. Following nationalization, Eddystone was renumbered 34028 and sent to Exmouth Junction. It became one of the first to be rebuilt in August 1958 and was then transferred to Bournemouth, where it worked services over the main line between Weymouth and Waterloo. It was also a regular performer on the Somerset and Dorset route to Bath, and in September 1962 it was

Eddystone was rebuilt and had its air-smooth casing removed for a more conventional look. It is seen here pulling a selection of coaches at the steam festival on the Bluebell railway in 2007.

transferred to Eastleigh. In May 1964 Eddystone was the first rebuilt Bulleid Light Pacific to be withdrawn and was sent to Barry scrap yard, South Wales, where it rested for the next 22 years. It was purchased by the Southern Pacific Rescue group and moved to a base at Sellindge near Ashford, Kent, for restoration and preservation.

• DARTMOOR

21C121 Dartmoor, West Country Class locomotive number 34021, was built at the Brighton works and entered service in January of 1946. It was rebuilt in December 1957, and just ten years later it was withdrawn and taken to the Barry scrap yard in South Wales.

At their steam day in 2007, to commemorate the fortieth anniversary of the end of Southern Rail steam on 9 July, 1967, the Bluebell Railway ran 34028 Eddystone in the guise of 34021 Dartmoor. It was one of the locomotives to operate on the last day, hauling a boat train from Southampton Docks to Waterloo.

Stroudley A1 Terrier

The London, Brighton and South Coast Railway (LBSCR) A1 Class 0-6-0T steam locomotives were generally known as Terriers. They were designed by William Stroudley, and their use was for hauling commuter trains, mainly in south and east London. When Stroudley came to office at the LBSCR at the beginning of 1870, he

Fenchurch has been a loyal servant of the Bluebell Railway line for some years now, having been delivered in 1964. For a number of years prior to this, she was celebrated as the oldest locomotive working on British Railways.

found that there was very little in the way of standardization among the locomotive stock, and saw the need for a small range of standard locomotives. In the following 15 years he would remedy this situation, designing a series of small standard steam locomotives, of which the class A1 Terrier was the smallest. The first batch of Terriers was started in 1872, and the building programme lasted until 1880.

By the 1890s the trackwork in the London area had been much improved, and with the extra requirement more powerful engines

Fenchurch had an overhaul during which it was converted back to represent its original A1 rather than A1X form. It returned to service in February 2001. The cab is light and functional with gauges in strategic positions, the top large gauge being a duel air pressure gauge for the main reservoir and brake pipe. Other controls include the accelerator handle on the right and the brake on the left. Internal work to the boiler was also carried out during overhaul, although the actual boiler itself was in good condition.

SPECIFICATIONS

Class:	A1
Year:	1872
Wheel arrangement:	0-6-0T
Cylinders:	2: 12 x 20 inch
Driving wheel diameter:	4 ft
Tractive effort:	7,650 lbs
Boiler pressure:	150 lbs
Valve gear:	Stephenson
Coal capacity:	18 cwt
Water capacity:	500 gallons

Stepney has been with the Bluebell Railway for quite some years, and never ceases to astonish both young and old. She has been modified to become a class A1X locomotive, which entailed fitting a Marsh boiler and an extended smoke box. She was also repainted into Stroudley's famous 'Improved Engine Green' gamboge livery.

were needed, thus leaving the little Terriers somewhat redundant. They were now moved to outlying areas to service the suburban lines, which they were ideally suited to.

By the beginning of the twentieth century, many were withdrawn and sent to scrap, due to less being required and the simple fact that they had outlived their lifespan. Those that did survive were found to be ideal when hooked up with the recently introduced push-pull 'motor-trains', even though they needed a certain amount of modifying.

At nationalization BR acquired several Terriers, and they put them to use on the Isle of Wight, KESR, Hayling Island branch, Brighton works, Littlehampton wharf and even on the GWR line at Weston,

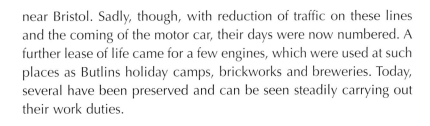

near Bristol. Sadly, though, with reduction of traffic on these lines and the coming of the motor car, their days were now numbered. A further lease of life came for a few engines, which were used at such places as Butlins holiday camps, brickworks and breweries. Today, several have been preserved and can be seen steadily carrying out their work duties.

• TERRIER 672 FENCHURCH

Fenchurch was sold to the Newhaven Harbour Company, being light enough to cross a bridge within the docks. It came back into

Even after more than 130 years, Stepney is seen quite happily carrying out her shunting duties at the Horsted Keynes depot.

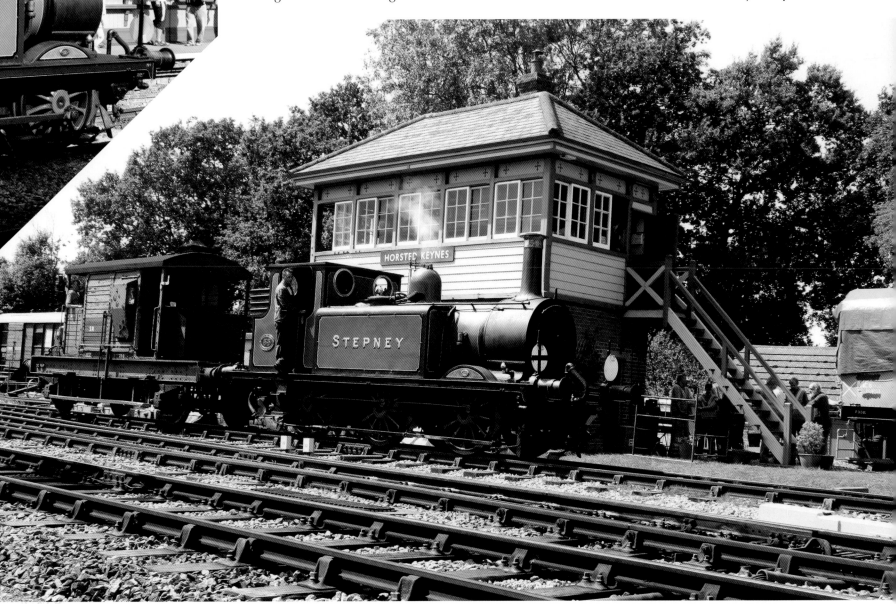

Southern Railway ownership, and continued for many years to work at Newhaven. It came to the Bluebell Line in 1964, having been a celebrity for a number of years, as the oldest locomotive working on British Railways.

• TERRIER 55 STEPNEY

In later years Stepney was particularly associated with the Hayling Island branch, until being sold to the Bluebell Railway in May 1960, as their first locomotive. It appeared in Reverend W. Awdry's Railway Series book, *Stepney the "Bluebell" Engine*.

Normally stationed at the Bressingham Museum in Norfolk, 'Martello', a Southern Railways Brighton Terrier, is seen while visiting the West Somerset Railway in 2007. Like Martello, many of these Terriers ended their lives at holiday camps, brickworks and breweries. The Westinghouse air-brake system (right) on Martello is not unique to that locomotive. The first of the Terriers to have the system fitted from new was Brighton/Newport, which also won the gold medal at the 1878 Paris Exhibition for her design, workmanship and finish.

Painted in its livery of Marsh Brown and Umber with LBSC (the London, Brighton and South Coast) lettering, Martello is seen steaming up at Minehead station in preparation for a busy steam weekend.

• TERRIER 662 MARTELLO

Martello entered service in October 1875, and it was still operational until 1961. In 1964 Martello was bought by Billy Butlin, cosmetically restored and then run at the Butlins holiday camp at Ayr until in 1971. It was then purchased by the Bressingham Museum, Norfolk, where it was in steam until the late 1970s. Terrier 662 was returned to steam in 2002 by the engineering department at Bressingham.

Drummond M7

The M7 Class 0-4-4 passenger tank locomotive was manufactured in the late nineteenth and early twentieth centuries. It was designed by Dugald Drummond for use on the intensive London network of the London and South Western Railway (LSWR).

This was the first locomotive to be designed by Drummond after he had replaced William Adams as Locomotive Superintendent of the LSWR in 1895. The design was an enlargement of the Adams T1 locomotive, with a sloping grate with greater area, which resulted in more power. It also became the heaviest 0-4-4 type ever run in Britain.

The first 25 examples came out of Nine Elms works between March and November of 1897, and although these locomotives had a long and successful life, several design changes occurred, and modifications were also made as the workload and requirements changed. A push-pull system was introduced after

Victorian-designed and Edwardian-built, M7 30053 – which is synonymous with the relaid Purbeck Line – returned to the Swanage Railway in 2007 after its major engineering overhaul, 20 years to the month since it triumphantly arrived back in the Isle of Purbeck after a 20-year stay in the USA.

30053 awaiting passengers on a beautiful spring morning at Corfe Castle station on the Swanage line in Dorset. It's difficult to miss the restoration work being carried out on the castle in the background.

1912, which was eventually replaced on 36 of the long-frames versions, due to occasional malfunction, with a more modern compressed air system.

In 1948 all but two locomotives came under the BR banner, and although they had been successful suburban line passenger engines under the LSWR and Southern Railway, newer and more modern engines were taking over that role, and so they were assigned branch line work. By 1963 most of the class was based at Bournemouth, working the Swanage branch, but here too modern locomotives would soon take over as part of the modernization plan, and by 1964 they were being withdrawn.

SPECIFICATIONS

Class:	M7
Year:	1897
Wheel arrangement:	0-4-4
Cylinders:	2: 18½ x 26 inch
Driving wheel diameter:	5 ft 7 inches
Tractive effort:	19,775 lbs
Boiler pressure:	175 lbs
Valve gear:	Stephenson
Coal capacity:	3 tons 5 cwt
Water capacity:	1,300 gallons

Maunsell Class V 'Schools'

The Southern Railways Class V, generally known as the 'Schools' class, was designed by Richard Maunsell, who became the Southern Railways' first CME after grouping in 1923. Generally understood to be the most powerful class of 4-4-0 in Britain, and possibly the world, it was also the last to use this wheel arrangement in Britain.

Always eagerly awaited is the 'Schools' class locomotive. It became very successful in its time and they probably rank as one of the finest 4-4-0s to run in Britain. This is Repton steaming up and ready to go.

The locomotives were all named after English Public Schools and ordered in two batches of ten and twenty, although the second batch was increased to thirty during construction. Only the first batch ran without smoke deflectors, which were added to those ten engines during 1932 to 1933.

Maunsell was required to design a new express passenger train for the Tonbridge to Hastings line, which suffered from heavy restrictions regarding the tunnels on the route, and also the sharp bends.

Much of the layout of the new locomotive took its cue from the current Lord Nelson 4-6-0 design, although a smaller engine was requested. A short wheelbase was decided on, along with a 4-4-0 wheel arrangement, and the cab was specifically profiled to deal with the restrictive gauge of the bridges and tunnels on that particular line. The first batch of ten engines came from the Eastleigh works in 1930, which were soon followed by a further 30.

SPECIFICATIONS

Class:	V
Year:	1934
Wheel arrangement:	4-4-0
Cylinders:	2: 16½ x 26 inch
Driving wheel diameter:	6 ft 7 inches
Tractive effort:	25,135 lbs
Boiler pressure:	220 lbs
Valve gear:	Walschaerts
Coal capacity:	5 tons
Water capacity:	4,000 gallons

The fastest recorded speed for these locomotives was 95 mph (152 kph), achieved by Repton in 1938 whilst pulling four coaches. However there is a drawback when you have such high power and relatively low weight – when starting the locomotive from a standstill, wheelslips frequently occur, calling for skilled handling on the footplate. Repton is seen here at a slightly more sedate speed on the Watercress line.

The initial Schools class livery was in Maunsell's darker version of the London and South Western Railway (LSWR) passenger sage green, lined in black and white. Numbers were positioned on the cab side and the word 'Southern' was placed on the tender, in yellow. During the Second World War the locomotives were painted black with yellow lettering and numbers, but this changed when Bulleid became CME, to malachite green with 'sunshine yellow' picking out the numbers, and the word 'Southern' painted on the tender. The locomotives were allocated numbers 900–939. After nationalization several paint schemes were used, and numbers took on the BR theme and became 30900-30939. Following modifications during their lifespan to improve performance, the class operated until 1963, after which mass withdrawal took place.

All 40 locomotives were named after English public schools, and where possible they were sent to a railway station near the specific school for official naming. Here, the pupils were allowed to visit the cab of their new locomotive.

30926 Repton, one of three preserved, was built at the Eastleigh works in May 1934 and ran until December 1962. It returned to Eastleigh works in April 1966 and was fully restored and out-shopped on 28 February 1967. Repton sailed to Montreal on the SS Roonah Head from Gladstone Dock, Liverpool in April 1967 and was displayed at Steamtown, Bellows Falls, Vermont until repatriated to the North Yorkshire Moors Railway on 11 April 1987. Once back in the UK, the engine was restored.

Resplendent in its Maunsell lined, Southern Railway olive green with yellow markings and 'Southern' writ large on the tender, 1638 is seen at Sheffield Park station on the Bluebell Railway in Sussex.

Maunsell U Class

The Southern Railway U Class 2-6-0 mogul steam locomotives were designed by Richard Maunsell for passenger duties on the Southern Railway cross-country and semi-fast express lines.

Several of the class were rebuilds of the K Class, and gained the nickname 'U-Boats'. They could operate over most of the Southern Railway network and survived until 1966, by which time all had been withdrawn.

1638 was out-shopped from Ashford works on 9 May 1931. She was initially allocated to Redhill but, following the electrification of the Brighton line in 1933, she was sent to Guildford. When she received her first overhaul in 1933, her number was changed from A638 to 1638, and at a second overhaul in 1935 she gained smoke deflectors. After a few moves, and a while in a siding at Eastleigh, 1947 saw her being re-steamed and returned to Exmouth junction.

After nationalization and a further overhaul she obtained her new BR number 31638, and in 1949 she ended her West Country life when sent to Stewarts Lane, Chatham. A number of moves then followed before she moved to Fratton, where she worked on the Portsmouth docks line until November 1959, when the Fratton shed was closed. 31638 then went to her final shed, Guildford, where she worked until January 1964, when she was sold to Barry scrap yard in South Wales. 31638 became the 114th engine to leave Barry, arriving at the Bluebell Railway on 30 July 1980.

Steaming up and ready to go, the driver of 1638 waits patiently for the signal to change and allow him to move out of the station. Three other U Class locomotives have survived – 1618, 1806 and 1625.

SPECIFICATIONS

Class:	U
Year:	1928
Wheel arrangement:	2-6-0
Cylinders:	2: 19 x 28 inch
Driving wheel diameter:	6 ft
Tractive effort:	23,866 lbs
Boiler pressure:	200 lbs
Valve gear:	Walschaerts
Coal capacity:	5 tons
Water capacity:	4,000 gallons

Wainwright 01 Class

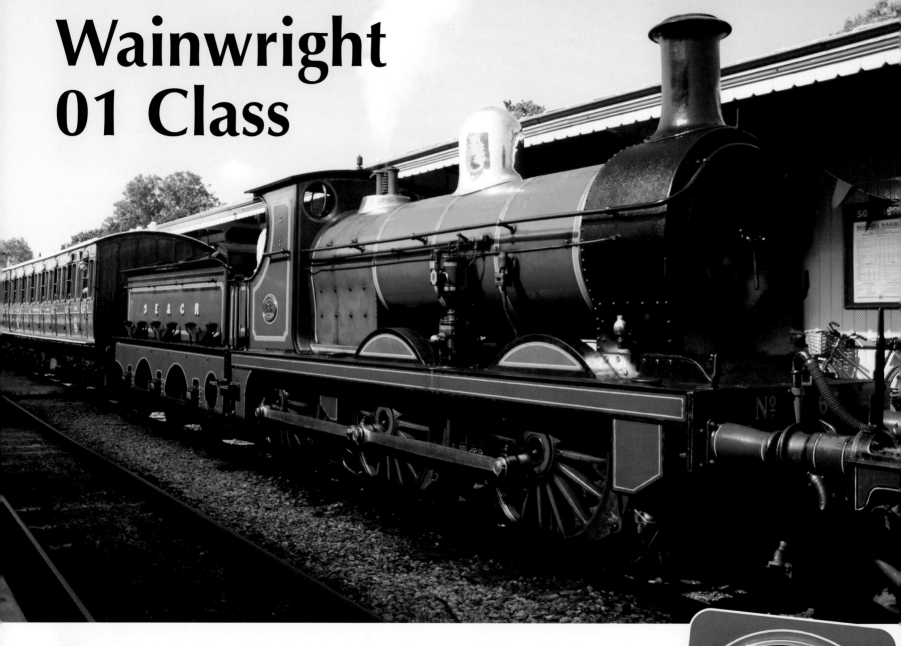

The South Eastern and Chatham Railway (SECR) O Class, and its rebuilt O1 Class derivative, was a class of 0-6-0 steam locomotives designed for freight work.

The modified O1 Class locomotives could be easily distinguished from the original O Class in that they didn't have the rounded cab, and an H-type boiler was fitted, which had a substantial dome. Harry Wainwright, who had been appointed Locomotive, Carriage and Wagon Superintendent of the SECR in 1899, was determined to

Having once spent a long time hidden away, it's good to see 65 (30165) in regular action. Here she is at Sheffield Park station, waiting for her passengers to board for their trip along the Bluebell Railway during 2007.

SOUTH EASTERN & CHATHAM RAILWAY
65
ASHFORD WORKS

bring standardization to the company stock, and this was just his starting point.

Due to the initial design of these locomotives, and the fact that they had very low axle weights, they could travel in many areas where heavier locomotives wouldn't dare go. As the SER and SECR were sensitive to this requirement, the O1s were ideal for these lines.

Number 65 was built at Ashford as an O Class locomotive and had its rebuild to Class O1 in 1908. Following the First World War, she was based at Ashford and between the two wars was regularly seen at Folkstone harbour with the number 1065. After nationalization she took on the number 31065, and again could be seen in the Ashford area right up to the 1950s, when withdrawals started. A last moment of glory came for 31065 when she double-headed with C Class 592, working the final service on the Hawkhurst branch.

Number 65 was not a Barry scrap yard engine, but was withdrawn from service by BR in 1961, at the time carrying number 31065. Condemned but not scrapped, she awaited her fate at Ashford. In 1963 she was purchased directly from BR, and is now a regular on the Bluebell Line in the county of East Sussex.

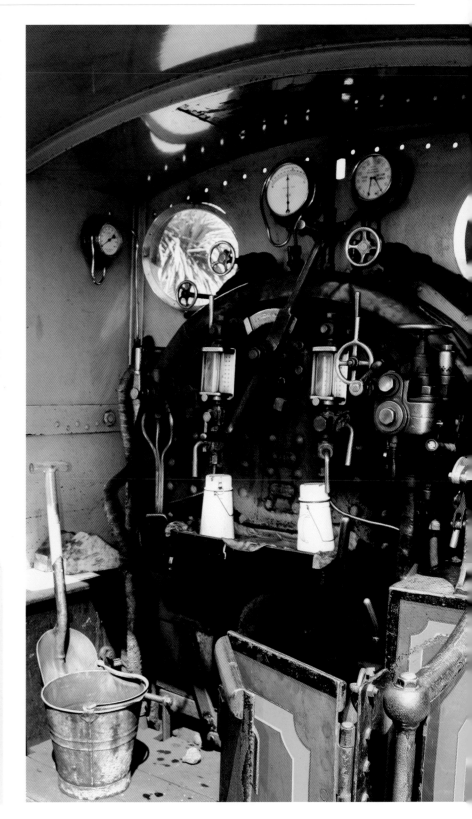

A view inside the cab of 65, showing the gauges and inspection instruments needed to make the train work. The firebox can be seen just behind the green door, and the red lever that makes the train move is in the centre. Dials at the top also show brake and boiler pressure.

SPECIFICATIONS

Class:	01
Year:	1896
Wheel arrangement:	0-6-0
Cylinders:	2: 18 x 26 inch
Driving wheel diameter:	5 ft 2 inches
Tractive effort:	17,300 lbs
Boiler pressure:	150 lbs
Valve gear:	Stephenson
Coal capacity:	2½ tons
Water capacity:	2,000 gallons

Bulleid Merchant Navy

Even today, people gasp with excitement when they see one of these class of locomotives come thundering into a station. It is difficult to imagine what they must have thought when they first went into service back in 1941. This was no ordinary steam locomotive – O. V. S. Bulleid saw to that when in 1937 he accepted the

35005 re-enacting one of the more famous boat trains from London Waterloo to Southampton Docks Ocean Terminal. 'The Cunarder' connected with the two Cunard Queens, RMS Queen Mary and RMS Queen Elizabeth, and the Cunard Line transatlantic service to New York, USA.

post of CME of the Southern Railway. In 1938 he was given approval to build the Merchant Navy class of modern 4-6-2 'Pacifics', which he packed full of innovative and modern equipment. The 'air-smoothed' casing was just the start of what this locomotive represented. Other innovations included chain-driven valve gear, an all-steel boiler equipped with thermic siphons within the firebox to promote better water circulation, rocking grate and hopper ashpan, and the cab layout was ergonomically designed to simplify operations.

The first, 21C1 Channel Packet, was built in 1941, and 29 more followed – three batches of ten were completed, the last being delivered by British Railways following nationalization. It was decided that this class of locomotive would be named after shipping companies serving the all-important Southampton Docks.

SPECIFICATIONS

Class:	8P
Year:	1941
Wheel arrangement:	4-6-2 (Pacific)
Cylinders:	3: 18 x 24 inches
Driving wheel diameter:	6 ft 2 inches
Tractive effort:	33,495 lbs
Boiler pressure:	250 psi
Valve gear:	Bulleid chain-drive; Walschaerts – 3 sets
Coal capacity:	5 tons
Water capacity:	5,200 gallons

In 1955 a rebuild of the first 15 of the class was ordered, which saw their 'air-smoothed' casing and chain-driven valve gear replaced, along with several other modifications. As successful as the modifications were, life for the Merchant Navy Class was short and it fell to the last member of the class, 35030 Elder-Dempster Lines, to haul the very last steam-hauled train – the 14.11 Weymouth-Waterloo on 9 July 1967. The next day, modern traction took over and there wasn't a breath of steam left in sight!

35005 Canadian Pacific ran from 13 October 1942 until withdrawal on 10 October 1965, with a rebuild in 1959. It spent from January 1966 until March 1973 at Barry scrap yard, when it was privately preserved at Carnforth, Lancashire.

Prior to its rebuild, Merchant Navy Class locomotive 35005 was a spectacle of modern technology in its air-smoothed casing (streamlining). This view from above shows just how, even after rebuild, it still had flowing lines.

Birth of the GWR

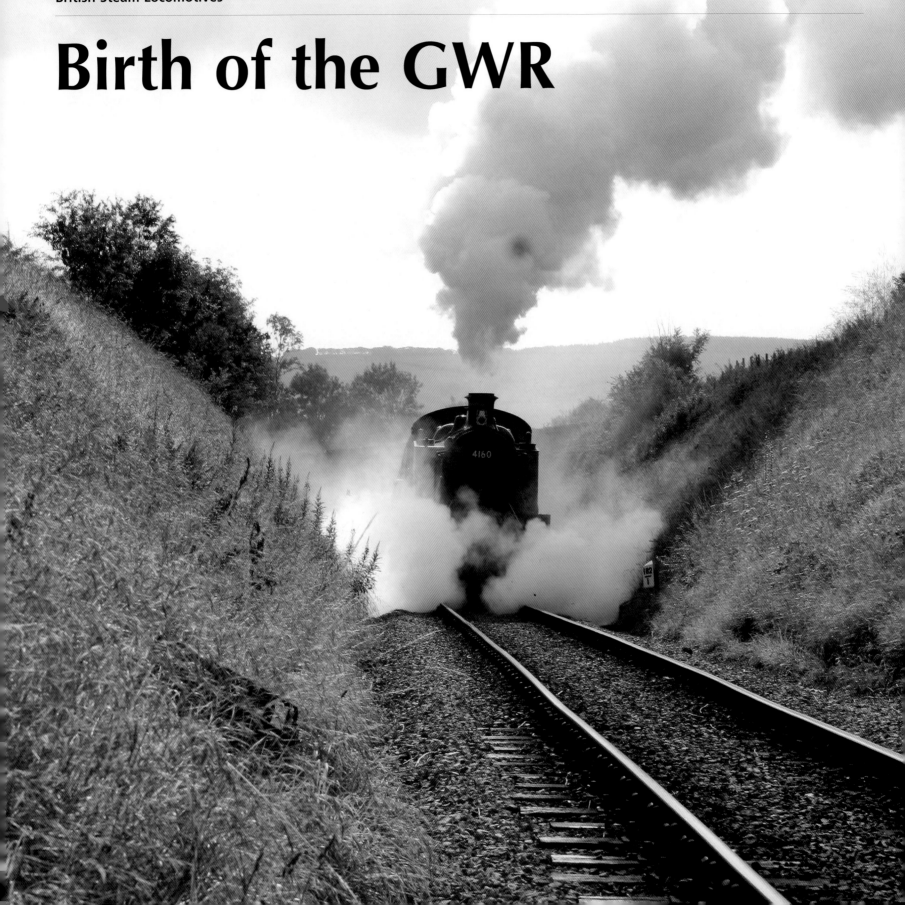

The Great Western Railway was founded in 1833 and managed to keep its identity during the 1923 grouping. It went on to become the Western Region section of British Railways when nationalization took place in 1948.

The constituent companies that made up the GWR at grouping were as follows:

Barry Railway

Cambrian Railways

Cardiff Railway

Rhymney Railway

Taff Vale Railway

Alexandra (Newport and South Wales) Docks and Railway

The narrow gauge Corris Railway was absorbed in 1930.

The total route length of the GWR was 3,800 miles (6,116 km). They also inherited locomotives: tenders 1,550, tanks 2,500; coaching vehicles 10,100; freight vehicles 90,000; electric vehicles 60; rail motor cars 70. Also inherited was 213 miles (343 km) of canals, 16 turbine and twin-screw steamers, plus several smaller vessels. Docks, harbours and equipment at Barry, Cardiff, Fishguard, Newport, Penarth, Plymouth, Port Talbot and several other places, along with ten hotels, were also included.

The company had quite a distinctive livery, with locomotives having middle chrome green above Indian red (later, plain black) frames.

The GWR was founded at a public meeting in Bristol in 1833, it was incorporated by an Act of Parliament in 1835, and Isambard Kingdom Brunel – its most famous father figure – was appointed engineer. Probably one of the most controversial decisions he made was to use a broad gauge line, when most others at the time were using a standard gauge. His thoughts were that this would allow the use of large wheels, providing smoother running at high speeds.

Broad gauge was later dropped after Parliament appointed a Gauge Commission, which duly moved in favour of standard gauge.

The first stretch of line, from London Paddington (also the London terminus today) to Taplow, near Maidenhead, opened in 1838. The full line to Bristol Temple Meads opened on completion of 'Box Tunnel' in 1841.

Collett 'Hall' Class

The 4900 Hall Class 4-6-0 are mixed traffic steam locomotives, which were designed by Charles Collett. A total of 259 were built, numbered 4900-99, 5900-99 and 6900-58.

Charles Benjamin Collett became Chief Mechanical Engineer of the GWR in 1922, and was asked to design a 4-6-0 to replace the

Hagley Hall seen at Kidderminster station during a steam gala at the Severn Valley Railway during 2007. Here, funds were also being collected for extensive work to be carried out on this beautiful locomotive.

SPECIFICATIONS

These figures are for the non-modified Halls.

Class:	4900 Hall
Year:	1928
Wheel arrangement:	4-6-0
Cylinders:	2: 18½ x 30 inch
Driving wheel diameter:	6 feet
Tractive effort:	27,275 lbs
Boiler pressure:	225 lbs
Valve gear:	Stephenson
Coal capacity:	6 tons
Water capacity:	4,000 gallons

Mogul 43xx Class. Initial work was carried out in 1924 on locomotive 2926 Saint Martin, of the 'Saint' Class, which became the prototype for the new class of engine. It was renumbered 4900 and spent three years in trials and being tampered with – a new 'Castle' type cab was fitted, the pitch of the boiler was altered, there was a reduction in the coupled wheel diameter, and outside steam pipes were added. These were just a few of the modifications and adjustments that led to what would become the new 'Hall' Class locomotive.

In a great cloud of smoke and lots of noise, Kinlet Hall double-heads with 2884 Class 3802, as they move off from Heywood station on the East Lancashire line.

Pitchford Hall accelerates away from Bewdley station on the Severn Valley Railway during a 2007 steam gala. Sadly, the Railway suffered enormous flood damage and the service only ran from here to Kidderminster.

Once Collett was happy with his new design, he placed an initial order of eighty with Swindon works, with the first batch of the new two-cylinder engines entering service in 1928. After the success of fourteen initial engines sent to the Cornish mainline, and by the time all of the first batch of eighty had been delivered in 1930, an order for a further 178 had already been placed. 150 engines could be seen in service by 1935 and the last of the class, 6958 Oxburgh Hall, was delivered in 1943.

Collett retired from the GWR at the age of seventy, and he was replaced by Frederick William Hawksworth in 1941, who went on to produce what is known as the 6959 Modified Hall Class. These

All hands to the controls as Kinlet Hall steams through the level-crossing on its way out of Ramsbottom station, continuing its return journey to Bury, Bolton street station.

appeared in 1944, and outwardly looked similar to the original Halls, but attention was focused on a higher level of superheating in the boiler to cope better with the inferior coal supplies of that period, and the introduction of full-length plate steel for the mainframes. These and other improvements were very successful and allowed the engine a freer movement and a better turn of speed, which led to these trains being nicknamed the 'greyhounds'. One further change was to the traditionally sculpted GWR tenders, which Hawksworth now changed to a straight-sided version.

Due to the post-war inferior coal supplies, the alternative of oil-firing was trialled. This was not a great success and the eleven that had been modified were returned to their normal coal-firing after a few years.

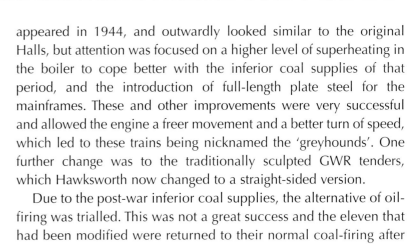

Looking at it here in 2007, you wouldn't know that Kinlet Hall could have survived a fall into a bomb crater, following a heavy German air-raid on Plymouth in 1941, which caused extensive damage to the bogie and mainframes.

Foremarke Hall was a development by Frederick Hawksworth of Charles Collett's earlier Hall Class and generally described as a Modified Hall Class. The first of these locomotives was outshopped from Swindon in 1944, carried plain black livery and was unnamed.

At nationalization in 1948, all but one of the Collett engines entered British Rail and were redesignated 5-MT. Sadly, 4911 Bowden Hall had been seriously damaged by a bomb during a raid by the German Luftwaffe and was therefore scrapped. Official withdrawal of the engines started in 1959, and by 1965 the last Hall Class locomotive had been taken out of service. Several of both the Hall and Modified Hall Classes have been preserved.

• 4930 HAGLEY HALL

Built May 1929. First shed allocation Wolverhampton, last shed allocation Swindon. Withdrawn December 1963. Acquired by Woodham's, Barry, May 1964. Sold to Severn Valley Railway, Bridgnorth, January 1973.

• 4953 PITCHFORD HALL

Built August 1929. First shed allocation Bristol, last shed allocation Cardiff East Dock. Withdrawn May 1963. Acquired by Woodham's, Barry, November 1963. Sold to DFR Norchard, February 1984.

4965 Rood Ashton Hall, seen carrying authentic GWR 1926 fully lined livery, is a regular main line performer, being the engine often used on the Shakespeare Express. The Sundays-only steam train service, which runs during the summer months (and occasionally at other times of the year), between Birmingham Snow Hill station and Stratford-upon-Avon (right) is a popular day out with young and old alike.

• 4936 KINLET HALL

Built June 1929. First shed allocation Chester, last shed allocation Cardiff East Dock. Withdrawn January 1964. Acquired by Woodham's, Barry, June 1964. Sold to G-WR, Toddington, May 1981.

• 4965 ROOD ASHTON HALL

Built November 1929. First shed allocation Wolverhampton, last shed allocation Didcot. Withdrawn March 1962. Scrapped at Swindon Works – or was she? The men in white coats at Tyseley Works, after much digging and delving, are absolutely convinced that one of their engines is most definitely not what they thought it was when they bought it! They say the time is now right to reveal to you that 'Albert Hall' is not 4983 at all, but is in reality 4965 'Rood Ashton Hall'.

MODIFIED HALL

• 7903 FOREMARKE HALL

Built April 1949. First shed allocation Old Oak Common, last shed allocation Cardiff East Dock. Withdrawn June 1964. Acquired by Woodham's, Barry, August 1964. Sold to SCR, Blunsdon June 1981.

Churchward 2800/2884 Class

The GWR 2800 Class was a heavy freight locomotive, the first 2-8-0 class in Great Britain, and was designed by George Jackson Churchward, CME of the GWR from 1902 to 1922.

The 2884 Class, also a heavy freight locomotive, was developed from the 2800, hence these are often classified together. They varied from the original design, though, with the most obvious feature being the Collett side-window cab. A long box was added

Seen on home territory, locomotive 3850 steams its way across the Somerset countryside, heading for Stogumber station on its way to Bishops Lydeard.

on the left side, along the running board, which was specifically for the storage of fire irons, a shield was positioned behind the whistle, and ATC was also installed.

The locomotive became so popular with the crews that after nationalization they requested British Rail build some more. Sadly, they were refused, and the standard 9F was chosen in their place, which saw the demise of these popular 2800 derivatives.

3850 was built at the Great Western Railway works in Swindon, and was introduced on 16 June 1942, in wartime black livery. Initially allocated to St Philip's Marsh, Bristol, it was put into storage

The prototype of the 2800 Class, number 97, was the first locomotive to operate in Britain with the 2-8-0 type of wheel arrangement. Sixteen have been preserved, but only a few of these are running.

SPECIFICATIONS

Class:	2884
Year:	1938
Wheel arrangement:	2-8-0
Cylinders:	2: 18 x 30 inch
Driving wheel diameter:	4 ft 7½ inches
Tractive effort:	35,380 lbs
Boiler pressure:	225 lbs
Valve gear:	Stephenson
Coal capacity:	6 tons
Water capacity:	3,500 gallons

With the beautiful Welsh countryside as a backdrop, locomotive 3802 transports its passengers to Carrog station on the Llangollen railway.

The 2884 Class, introduced in 1938, modified by C. B. Collett, had a number of alterations, which included outside steam pipes, and the cab was fitted with side-windows.

in 1958 after two further moves. In 1959 it was brought out of storage and moved to Aberdare, where it remained until 1963. Next came a number of additional moves, during which time it worked hauling coal and mineral trains, with the odd outing thrown in. A postal service was next on the agenda, before 3850 was taken out of service in August 1965, ending up at the Barry scrap yard later that same year.

The 38xx Preservation Society brought the locomotive to Minehead in 1984, where the long process of restoration began. In 2003 it was taken to Tyseley in Birmingham for final restoration work, and after two and a half years the locomotive was returned to the West Somerset Railway on 2 February 2006.

Locomotive 3802 is seen double heading with a Hall Class locomotive, awaiting passengers at the East Lancashire Bury Bolton street station (above). The two locomotives are making their way through the railway crossing at Ramsbottom (left) on their return journey from Rawtenstall. A good view of the cabs can be seen from the bridge just beyond the station. The busy signal box is just in view on the left.

Collett Manor Class

The GWR 7800 4-6-0 Manor Class locomotives were designed as a lighter version of the GWR Grange Class, and like the Granges they used parts from the GWR 4300 Class Moguls in the first twenty, built between 1938 and 1939. British Railways added a further ten in 1950.

7800 Torquay Manor was the first example built and went into service in January 1938. With the initial twenty built by February 1939, a further twenty were scheduled to follow, but with the Second World War now occupying people's minds, they were cancelled. The first batch was sent to depots at Wolverhampton, Bristol, Gloucester, Shrewsbury, Westbury in Wiltshire and Neyland in South Wales.

7822 Foxcote Manor is seen steaming its way through the Welsh countryside on its way to Carrog station. This is familiar territory for this locomotive, which spent its whole working life in Shropshire, Cheshire and North and Mid Wales.

SPECIFICATIONS

Class:	7800 Manor
Year:	1938
Wheel arrangement:	4-6-0
Cylinders:	2: 18 x 30 inch
Driving wheel diameter:	5 ft 8 inches
Tractive effort:	27,340 lbs
Boiler pressure:	225 lbs
Valve gear:	Stephenson
Coal capacity:	6 tons
Water capacity:	3,500 gallons

Following the end of the war and with nationalization now a fact, the Western region was given the go-ahead to build ten more Manor class locomotives, and numbers 7820-29 were shipped out from Swindon works in November and December of 1950. In the following years, several necessary minor alterations and modifications were carried out.

Undoubtedly, the most prestigious work they carried out was on the Cambrian Coast Express, which after taking over from a King or Castle at Shrewsbury, they went through to Aberystwyth.

The first of the class to be scrapped was 7809 Childrey Manor, withdrawn from Shrewsbury depot in April 1963 and cut up at Swindon. The final two, 7808 Cookham Manor and 7829 Ramsbury Manor, were condemned in December 1965.

At Llangollen station, Wales, locomotive Foxcote Manor makes its way past its complement of coaches. After changing tracks it will hook up to the coaches, and within a little while both will be on their way up the Welsh valley.

Ditcheat Manor exits the maintenance shed at Loughborough on the Great Central railway during 2005, soon after extensive work had been carried out.

• 7821 DITCHEAT MANOR

Built November 1950. First shed allocation Oswestry, last shed allocation Shrewsbury. Withdrawn November 1965. Barry scrap yard May 1966. Fifteen years later it was rescued by the Gloucester and Warwickshire Railway. After much restoration, it now regularly runs on the Llangollen railway.

• 7822 FOXCOTE MANOR

Built December 1950. First shed allocation Oswestry, last shed allocation Shrewsbury. Withdrawn November 1965. Barry scrap yard May 1966. Sold to Llangollen Railway, 1975. Restored 1987.

Collett 6400 Class

The GWR 6400 0-6-0 Class pannier tank steam locomotives were introduced by Charles Collett in 1932. They were closely related to the earlier 5400 Class and were a development of the Armstrong 1874 GWR 850 Class and the Dean 1891 GWR 2021 Class.

Forty were built, all out of the Swindon works, and they became very successful. They carried out both freight and light passenger work, and were capable of rapid acceleration and a reasonably high speed.

This class was primarily intended for light passenger work and was capable of rapid acceleration and reasonably high speed. 6430 was first allocated to Kidderminster, moving to Pontypool Road. Its final allocation was Yeovil, and it was withdrawn in October 1964.

6430 was built at Swindon in 1937 as part of lot number 305. The class spent their lives working many of the minor branch lines on the former GWR system, particularly the South Wales valleys, and were fitted for auto train working.

6430 was withdrawn in 1964; it was sold as scrap, but then re-sold to the Dart Valley Railway as a source of spares.

When the remains of the engine were purchased by its current owner in 1990, it represented an incomplete kit of parts. It spent some time undergoing restoration at Long Marston MOD depot, before moving on to Llangollen in 1996. Major restoration was then carried out over a period of eight years by a skilled and dedicated team, and 6430 moved under its own steam again in December 2003. An ex-GWR auto trailer coach will see 6430 portraying a branch line train of the 1940s.

6430 is a push-pull pannier tank locomotive of GWR origin. The class spent its life working many of the minor branch lines on the former GWR system, particularly the South Wales valleys, and was fitted for auto train working, as demonstrated here.

SPECIFICATIONS

Class:	6400
Year:	1932
Wheel arrangement:	0-6-0PT
Cylinders:	2: 16½ x 24 inch
Driving wheel diameter:	4 ft 7½ inches
Tractive effort:	16,510 lbs
Boiler pressure:	165 lbs
Valve gear:	Stephenson
Coal capacity:	3 tons
Water capacity:	1,100 gallons

Churchward 3700 City Class

The GWR 3700 4-4-0 City Class locomotives, designed by George Jackson Churchward, were designed specifically for hauling express passenger trains. There were twenty in total; ten were rebuilt from Atbara Class engines, of which the first, 3405, was converted in September 1902, the rest following between 1907 and 1909. The other ten were built as new during 1903 at the GWR's Swindon locomotive works. The whole class was gradually replaced and scrapped between 1927 and 1931.

The most famous in this class, 3440 City of Truro, was built at the GWR Swindon works in 1903. Subsequently renumbered 3717 in

A lot of huffing and puffing from City of Truro as she steams up early one spring morning ready for the weekend steam gala. 2007 saw her making many visits to a selection of lines around the country, where she was greeted with applause and excitement.

The 4-4-0 configuration used in Britain was primarily favoured for passenger services, although several types were used for mixed traffic in later years. The first British locomotives to use a 4-4-0 wheel layout were designed by William Bouch in 1860 for the Stockton & Darlington Railway.

Steam pours out from all directions as City of Truro picks up power and speed while moving out of Toddington station on the Gloucestershire and Warwickshire Railway in 2007.

SPECIFICATIONS

Class:	City
Year:	1903
Wheel arrangement:	4-4-0
Cylinders:	2: 18 x 26 inch
Driving wheel diameter:	6 ft 8½ inches
Tractive effort:	17,790 lbs
Boiler pressure:	200 lbs
Valve gear:	Stephenson
Coal capacity:	5 tons
Water capacity:	3,500 gallons

Seen above is City of Truro steaming its way through the Gloucestershire countryside on its way to Cheltenham race course, where its journey will end. The story about its famous run at over 100 mph (160 kph) back in 1904, way before Flying Scotsman achieved its personal best and broke the 100 mph barrier, still intrigues many even today. Whatever the case, she is a fine locomotive and deserves all the honours.

1912, it was reputedly the first steam locomotive in Europe to top the 100 mph (160 km/h) barrier – reportedly timed at the heady speed of 102.3 mph (164 km/h) ahead of the 'Ocean Mails' special from Plymouth to London Paddington on 9 May 1904.

Keeping in mind their reputation for safety, and even though the speed was recorded from the footplate, the railway company only allowed the overall timings to be put in print, not the actual figure, and therefore the speed was not published until 1907. Even then, there should have been two timekeepers, not just the one, but it is understood to have exceeded the 100 mph barrier.

In 1931 it was withdrawn from service and was subsequently bought by the London and North Eastern Railway, going on display at a newly built museum in York.

In 1957 British Rail returned it to service pulling special excursion trains and also using it for general everyday services. Based at Didcot, it reverted back to its original number 3440, and served the Newbury and Southampton branch line.

Retirement came once again in 1961, when it was exhibited at the National Railway Museum in York. It was lovingly restored in 1984 to take part in the 150th anniversary celebrations of the Great Western Railway. Recently, City of Truro has had major restoration work carried out to bring it back to full working order, to celebrate its great record-breaking achievement one hundred years earlier.

City of Truro makes a quick stop to take on a tank full of water at Winchcombe station on the Gloucestershire and Warwickshire railway line.

Churchward/Collett 4500/4575 Classes

Prototype locomotive 2-6-2T, number 115, introduced in 1904 by George Jackson Churchward, was the forerunner of the 4500 Class locomotives that served the GWR for so long. This initial engine performed so well that a further ten were ordered from the Wolverhampton works, their copper-topped chimneys gleaming as they exited the workshops. The Great Western branch lines could be steep in places and quite twisty, in particular in the West Country, but these little locomotives coped well with their superior acceleration. There was only one thing that hindered their performance, and that was the 4 ft 1½ inch wheels, although these

Described by many as the ideal branch-line locomotive, the 'Small Prairie' was normally painted in unlined green livery during its GWR days. Seen here in all her splendour is preserved number 5542 outside the maintenance shed at Toddington.

Superceding the 4400 Class engines in 1906 were the 4500 locomotives. These took all the best features from their predecessor and added, for example, larger driving wheels. 5542 can be seen pulling a complement of carriages on its familiar Gloucestershire and Warwickshire railway line (above). The once straight-backed bunker of the early 4400s was modified to have a curved shape, thus giving a larger capacity, as seen on this 4575 Class engine (below).

SPECIFICATIONS

Class:	4575
Year:	1924
Wheel arrangement:	2-6-2
Cylinders:	2: 17 x 24 inch
Driving wheel diameter:	4 feet 7½ inches
Tractive effort:	21,250 lbs
Boiler pressure:	200 lbs
Valve gear:	Stephenson
Coal capacity:	3 tons 14 cwt
Water capacity:	1,300 gallons

were changed for larger 4 ft 7½ inch versions on later models. As ever, though, modifications were made with particular attention being given to extra coal capacity, a superheated boiler with increased pressure and more cylinder capacity.

By 1906 more of these excellent engines were requested and, now classed 4500, they came with all the modifications. Apart from the first twenty, all were now built at the Swindon works, over a period of eighteen years up until 1924.

Churchward had, by 1921, retired from the GWR, and the man who took his place as CME was Charles Benjamin Collett. He kept faith in the engines and made more modifications, such as adding sloping side-tanks, which the new batch of engines inherited. These were numbered 4575-5574 (now given the 4575 Class) and were built between 1927 and 1929.

These locomotives became so popular that they could be seen on most GWR lines, and they were capable of all types of work, from the mundane pick-up freight duties to use on several well-known trains, which included hauling the Cambrian Coast Express and shuttling the Cheltenham Flyer.

The first withdrawal of the 4500 Class was 4531 in February 1950, while 4564 was still in service up until September 1964.

5542 is a 4575 Class locomotive, the last development of these pleasant engines designed by George Jackson Churchward.

Seen here in 2007, parked at Kidderminster station on the Severn Valley railway, is 4500 Class engine 4566 (left). It wouldn't be too long before it was mated with a series of carriages to make up the train which would travel along the line to Bewdley (below). This is the cab of locomotive 4566 (right).

A fascinating site – 5553 steams heavily at the start of the day, in preparation for the journeys it will cover during the steam weekend at the West Somerset railway. She is seen here at the main terminus at Minehead.

From the original design by Churchward in 1906, 5553 was one of the later batches modified by Collett to increase the size of the water tanks by 300 gallons.

Hooked up and ready to take her passengers to Bishops Lydeard, 5553 moves away from the platform in a cloud of smoke.

These locomotives were designed for light passenger and goods traffic. They were known as 'Small Prairies' – Prairie being the name given to the 2-6-2 wheel arrangement – because they were smaller than the first GWR tank locomotives to be built with this wheel arrangement. 5542 was built in 1928 and withdrawn in 1961. It was purchased in 1975 and restored at the West Somerset Railway.

4566 was built in October 1924, allocated Newton Abbot as the first shed and retired from Laira in April 1962, having served at St Ives and Penzance.

5553 was one of the later batches modified by Collett to increase the size of the water tanks. Built in November 1928, 5553 spent until February 1959 allocated to Bristol Bath Road, then transferred to Machynlleth for work on the Cambrian Coast Line. It was transferred to St Blazey in January 1961, and was withdrawn from there in November 1961. 5553 holds the record as the longest resident in Barry scrap yard, having arrived in March 1962 and having its final departure on 31 January 1990.

Collett 1400 Class

This class of locomotive was built by the GWR for use with 'auto trailers' for local branch line passenger trains. The designer was Charles B. Collett, they were introduced in 1932, and a total of 75 were built. These locomotives were originally numbered 4800-4874, but were later renumbered 1400-1474 between October and December 1946. Besides the normal working procedure from the cab, these locomotives could be worked by the driver from a driving compartment at one end of the 'auto coach', the controls being connected to the locomotive, where the fireman would be present. The locomotive stayed coupled to the coach, pushing it or pulling it, depending on which way it was facing – hence the term 'push-pull' was often applied to this configuration.

A busy Bishops Lydeard station, where locomotive 1450 awaits its passengers. Behind the locomotive is autocoach 178. These two vehicles are a pair, and generally based at the Dean Forest railway in the Forest of Dean, Gloucestershire.

There are four survivors of the class – numbers 1450, 1466, 1420 and 1442. 1450, seen here, was a long-serving locomotive on the 'Marlow Donkey' (Marlow-Bourne End), although most of its 30-year career was spent in Oxfordshire.

SPECIFICATIONS

Class:	1400
Year:	1932
Wheel arrangement:	0-4-2T
Cylinders:	2: 16 x 24 inch
Driving wheel diameter:	5 ft 2 inches
Tractive effort:	13,900 lbs
Boiler pressure:	165 lbs
Valve gear:	Stephenson
Coal capacity:	2 tons 13 cwt
Water capacity:	800 gallons

These engines were designed to replace the Wolverhampton 517 Class, now looking a little past their sell-by date. The design leaned very heavily on that of its predecessor, but was brought up to date. For example, a Group 7 SS type boiler was installed, and the cab was fitted with large windows front and rear.

Sadly, with the introduction of the diesel engine and the closure of branch lines, these little locomotives were no longer required, and withdrawal commenced in February 1956, with the last two being taken out of service in May 1965.

1450 was built at Swindon as 4850 in July 1935, and from then until 1950 it was a regular performer on the Abingdon, Fairford and Woodstock branches. It then transferred to Slough to work the Windsor and Marlow branches, returning to Oxford in 1959. 1450 was then variously based at Exeter, Taunton, Yeovil and Exmouth, where it was withdrawn. This was one of two engines which were the last of their class in service. In 1965, 1450 was sold out of service to the Dart Valley Railway.

British Rail 1948-1994

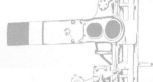

British Railways, later trading under the name of British Rail, took over the running of the British Rail network in 1948, amalgamating the 'Big Four' railway companies and all their component parts. Robert Riddles was appointed chief engineer, and it would be his designs that would standardize the next generation of locomotives, coaches and wagons – the idea was to have standardization of parts and fittings, along with ease of maintenance, across the range.

Between 'Nationalization' in 1948 through to 'Privatization', brought in under John Major's Conservative government's Railways Act of 1993, 999 BR standard locomotives were built in 12 different types. These ranged from the 2MT 2-6-0 and 2-6-2 tank classes, through to the powerful Class 9F heavy goods 2-10-0, and Britannia Class express passenger 4-6-2.

During this period, a huge change happened on the railways of Britain, with steam locomotives being phased out and replaced by the new diesel and electric-powered engines. People were now the major concern rather than freight, and at the same time the whole network was severely rationalized.

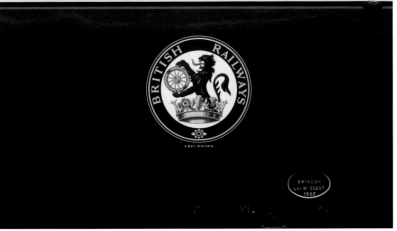

Eastern Region (ER) – southern LNER lines

North Eastern Region (NER) – northern LNER lines
in England and all ex-LMS lines east of Skipton

London Midland Region (LMR) – LMS lines in
England and Wales and most ex-LNER lines
west of Skipton

Scottish Region (ScR) – LMS and LNER lines
in Scotland

Southern Region (SR) – SR lines

Western Region (WR) – GWR lines

The country was now split into six main regions of operation. Although these regions formed the basis of the BR business structure until the 1980s, regional boundaries were re-drawn on a few occasions in the 1950s, to make them more geographically based rather than being based on pre-nationalization ownership. The North Eastern Region was merged with the Eastern Region in the 1960s, and a new Anglia Region was split off from the Eastern Region in the 1980s.

Standard Class 2

The British Railways Standard Class 2 2-6-0 moguls were a direct development of the earlier LMS Class 2MT 2-6-0. Sixty-five of this class were built at North Road Shops, Darlington works in the 1950s. As a small tender locomotive, designed to haul both passenger and goods trains, they were ideal for cross-country and branch-line work, and thus could be seen in many parts of Britain.

Compared to their LMS predecessor, they had a reduced-sized cab fitted, therefore allowing them to comply with the loading gauge. Along with other standard fittings, such as a taller chimney, these locomotives used a BR3 type tender, and some were even fitted with a speedometer. Fondly nicknamed 'Mickey Mouse', the last of the class, 78064, was completed in 1956, but withdrawals started very soon after.

78019 was completed in March 1954 and was initially based at Kirkby Stephen, spending the following six years working the lines

78019 was purchased privately by a member of the Severn Valley railway and arrived at Bridgnorth in 1973. It was moved to the GCR (Great Central Railway) in 1998 for restoration, after which it ran services on that and other lines.

through the Pennines and the Lake District. As lines started to close, the engine gradually made its way south. It spent time at Wigan Springs Branch, Northwich and Willesden in London, before heading north to Nuneaton, and finally to the Crewe south shed. Withdrawal came in November 1966, and a move to Barry scrap yard happened the following year, where it spent the next six years. After being purchased privately, it moved to the Severn Valley Railway in 1973.

Steaming out of Loughborough station on the GCR, 78019 hauls its carriage-load of passengers through the goods yard to the next stop at Quorn and Woodhouse station.

SPECIFICATIONS

Class:	2MT
Year:	1954
Wheel arrangement:	2-6-0
Cylinders:	2: 16½ x 24 inch
Driving wheel diameter:	5 ft
Tractive effort:	18,513 lbs
Boiler pressure:	200 lbs
Valve gear:	Walschaerts
Coal capacity:	4 tons
Water capacity:	3,000 gallons

Standard Class 4

British Railways Standard Class 4 2-6-0 locomotives were designed at the ex-LNER works at Doncaster, who also went on to build 70 of the 115 built – the last in the series, 76114, also became the last steam engine to come out of the Doncaster

works. The remainder was constructed at the ex-Lancashire and Yorkshire works at Horwich.

Taking its basic design from the LMS Ivatt Class 4, its 5 ft 3 in diameter driving wheels and its lightweight axle load made the

In 2007, 'Pocket Rocket' 76079, as it was known, became the first steam locomotive to run from the main line at Wareham Down to Corfe Castle and Swanage since Sunday 18 June, 1967.

The Swanage Railway is situated on the Isle of Purbeck, and runs from Swanage to Norden in the south-east corner of the picturesque county of Dorset. Seen here is Locomotive 76079 on its way to Norden station.

locomotive ideally suited to freight work, with virtually unrestricted route availability.

A selection of 35 examples was sent to Scotland to cover the Scottish Region, which worked the route between Carlisle and Harwick, others also working the Dumfries to Stranraer coastal section. For the Southern Region, 37 made their way to the Eastleigh, Southampton and Bournemouth area, covering services as far apart as Portsmouth, Redhill and Swanage, the Lymington

SPECIFICATIONS

Class:	4MT
Year:	1952
Wheel arrangement:	2-6-0
Cylinders:	2: 17½ x 26 inch
Driving wheel diameter:	5 ft 3 inches
Tractive effort:	24,170 lbs
Boiler pressure:	225 lbs
Valve gear:	Walschaerts
Coal capacity:	6 tons
Water capacity:	3,500 gallons

BR built 80 of this 4-6-0 'mixed traffic' design. 75029 was the first of the class to be built with a double chimney, thus improving an already well-regarded design.

Boat Train to London Waterloo being the most prestigious of all the services. For the Northern Region they were dispersed all over, from Darlington to Hull and down to York, not only as passenger trains but coal trains too.

Most of the London Midland Region's batch of 15 spent their working lives in the Liverpool, Manchester and Preston areas, while the Eastern Region divided its allotted 15 between two London depots – five to Stratford and the remainder to Neasden. The first to be withdrawn was 76028 on 31 May 1964, and the last four were withdrawn on 31 December 1967 from Wigan Springs Branch shed.

76079 was built at the British Railways Horwich works and was allocated shed 10D Bolton Plodder Lane. Withdrawal came on 31 December 1967 as one of the last four from 10A Wigan Springs Branch shed.

SPECIFICATIONS

Class:	4MT
Year:	1951
Wheel arrangement:	4-6-0
Cylinders:	2: 18 x 28 inch
Driving wheel diameter:	5 ft 8 inches
Tractive effort:	25,500 lbs
Boiler pressure:	225 lbs
Valve gear:	Walschaerts
Coal capacity:	6 tons
Water capacity:	3,500 gallons

The British Railways Standard Class 4 4-6-0 locomotives were built during the 1950s and were designed for mixed traffic and use on secondary lines, where the Class 5s were too heavy to travel.

The design was carried out by R. A. Riddles at Brighton on the south coast, but with assistance from Swindon, Derby and Doncaster works; construction was carried out at the Swindon works. The class of 80 lightweight 4-6-0 locomotives worked both goods and passenger services on virtually any secondary route.

The first engine was put into service in May 1951, and resembled a tender version of the LMS 2-6-4 tanks built by Stanier and

75029, Green Knight, spent most of its life on the Cambrian lines. It is seen here at Grosmont station on the North Yorkshire Moors.

Fairburn. These engines replaced many of the older and now obsolete types and clocked up high mileage, covering many different areas with both freight and passenger work. As good as they were, the modernization plans of 1955 saw the start of their replacement and the first withdrawal, 75067, took place on 31 October 1964 from the Eastleigh shed.

75029 was built at the Swindon works and entered operational service in 1954. In 1957 it was fitted, experimentally at the time, with a double blastpipe and chimney. It was withdrawn from service in 1967, and was immediately purchased for preservation. The locomotive was bought in 1998 with the intention that it was to be operated by NYMR on hire, once overhauled. On completion of this

Having gone through a recent major overhaul, it is good to see 80002 back in traffic. Here she is seen double-heading out of Keighley station on the KWR line in 2007.

When decommissioned, 80078 remained at Barry scrap yard for 10 years before being purchased by the Southern Steam Trust in 1976. Restoration started in 1978, and she now makes regular visits to many of the Heritage lines.

overhaul, it entered service on NYMR in May 2000. In November 2002, the locomotive was withdrawn from service, once again for overhaul. With this nearly complete, the locomotive returned to NYMR in November 2005. NYMR then completed any outstanding works themselves, and put the locomotive back into service on 10 February 2006.

When British Railways took charge of the railways on nationalization in 1948, it was noted that although the London Midland Region and the Western Region had a number of 2-6-2 and 2-6-4 tank engines, Scotland and the Southern Region were struggling through with very old pre-grouping stock.

BR therefore decided to build the Class 4 tank engine, which took much of its design from the LMS Fairburn 2-6-4T. These too had a history, having been based on the LMS Stanier 2-6-4T, which in turn was based on an earlier Fowler 2-6-4T. The new locomotives had

SPECIFICATIONS

Class:	4MT
Year:	1951
Wheel arrangement:	2-6-4T
Cylinders:	2: 18 x 28 inch
Driving wheel diameter:	5 ft 8 inches
Tractive effort:	25,100 lbs
Boiler pressure:	225 lbs
Valve gear:	Walschaerts
Coal capacity:	3 tons
Water capacity:	2,000 gallons

smaller cylinders and higher pressure boilers, were more economical in operation and became popular with footplate crews for their better running and improved cab facilities.

The design was undertaken at Brighton, where 90 of the class were also built, with R. A. Riddles overseeing the project. The main modifications were a reduction to their envelope so that they would comply with the L1 loading gauge, and so the tank and cab had a much rounder shape than the Fairburn engine. The new locomotives were classified as 4MT on the Eastern, Midland and Scottish

Regions, but their Southern Region classification was 4P/4F. The majority worked on the Central and South Western sections of the Southern Region, the LTSR lines of the Eastern Region and the Glasgow commuter lines in Scotland.

Besides the 90 built at Brighton, a further 15 were manufactured at the Derby works and ten more at the Doncaster works. Fifteen more were scheduled to be built but, due to the impending introduction of the diesel, these were cancelled. Built between 1951 and 1956, a total of 115 were manufactured, of which the first to be introduced

Sister locomotive to 80078 is 80104, whose restoration was completed in 1997. Both these engines operate regularly on the Swanage railway.

80135 is the only Class 4MT preserved in British Rail green livery. No 4MTs ran in British Rail green while in mainline service.

was 80010. These tank engines served all regions except the Western, and were particularly associated with the London, Tilbury and Southend line, where they shipped commuters back and forth until electrification in 1962. After this, they were gradually moved to outlying areas before being withdrawn throughout the 1960s.

The first locomotive withdrawn was 80040 on 6 May 1964 from Exmouth Junction shed.

80002 was built on 17 October 1952 at the British Rail Derby works. It was withdrawn on 1 March 1967, with its last shed being Polmadie.

80078 was built on 2 February 1954 at the British Railways Brighton works. Its first shed allocation was Plaistow, and it was withdrawn from shed 84B Croes Newydd on 24 July 1965.

80104 was built on 31 March 1955 at the British Railways Brighton works. Its first shed allocation was 33A Plaistow, and it was withdrawn from shed 89C Machynlleth on 24 July 1965.

80135 was built on 30 April 1956 at the British Railways Brighton works. Its first shed allocation was Plaistow, and it was withdrawn from Shrewsbury on 24 July 1965.

Standard Class 5

The Standard Class 5MT 4-6-0 built by British Railways in the 1950s, of which 172 examples were produced, was essentially a development of the William Stanier LMS 'Black 5' locomotive – probably the most successful mixed traffic locomotive in Britain. By taking this design and bringing it up to date with all the latest ideas, a new Standard Class 5 locomotive was born.

The design for the new locomotive was carried out at the ex-LNER Doncaster works, overseen by R. A. Riddles, CME at the time, while most of the actual construction took place at the BR Derby works.

A brief stop for 73096 while she takes on water at Ropley station on the Watercress line – Mid Hants railway in 2007.

73096 underwent restoration at Ropley – completed in October 1993 – with a new tender being constructed on an ex-LMS Stanier 'Black 5' tender chassis. Originally restored as 73080 Merlin and painted in BR lined black livery, the locomotive was subsequently renumbered 73096 and was also repainted in BR lined green, a livery first applied when the engine was allocated to Shrewsbury in 1958.

SPECIFICATIONS

Class:	5MT
Year:	1951
Wheel arrangement:	4-6-0
Cylinders:	2: 19 x 28 inch
Driving wheel diameter:	6 ft 2 inches
Tractive effort:	26,120 lbs
Boiler pressure:	225 lbs
Valve gear:	Walschaerts
Coal capacity:	49 tons 3 cwt – 55 tons 5 cwt
Water capacity:	4,200 gallons – 5,650 gallons

It is interesting to note that numbers 73125-73154 were built with the Italian-influenced Caprotti rotary cam poppet valve gear.

The new design incorporated a type 3B boiler, higher running plate and larger driving wheels, which were increased by two inches, and a standard cab to keep in line with the other classes.

April 1951 saw the first of the class introduced, 73000, but by January of 1952 there were already 30 in service. A gap of about three years passed before Derby works commenced building the next batch of these locomotives, which started in August of 1955. A further 100 were then built up to 1957, with 42 of these being built at the Doncaster works.

Seen here is locomotive 73129, which is the only surviving Standard Class 5 built by British Railways fitted with the Italian-influenced Caprotti valve gear.

The first withdrawal, 73027, was on 29 February 1964 from Swindon shed, and the last locomotive to go was 73069 on 18 August 1968 from Carnforth shed.

73096 was built at the Derby works in 1955 and allocated to the Patricroft (Manchester) shed, also spending time at Shrewsbury.

Gloucester and Nuneaton until withdrawn from service in 1967, and ending up at Barry scrap yard. It remained there until 1985, when it was rescued for restoration, which was completed in October 1993, along with a new tender being constructed. Restored as number 73080 Merlin and painted in BR lined black livery, it was subsequently renumbered 73096, while also being repainted in BR lined green.

73129 is the sole survivor of the last batch of 30 to be built at Derby works in August 1956, and is unique in being the only preserved Standard Class 5 fitted with Caprotti valve gear. Allocated to shed 84G Shrewsbury in September 1958, she moved to Patricroft (Manchester) shed, spending the remainder of her working life there, before being withdrawn in December 1967.

From Barry scrap yard she was purchased, together with the tender from 75079, by Derby Corporation in 1972, as a potential exhibit for the Midland Railway Project. Some years on, 73129 was restored and back in working order.

A special moment is captured as 73129 is seen at full steam pulling her complement of carriages on her return journey to Swanage station.

Standard Class 9

The BR Standard Class 9F 2-10-0 was designed by Robert Riddles and was the last in a series of standardized locomotive classes designed for British Railways during the 1950s.

Fast, and one of the most powerful engines ever constructed in Britain, these locomotives were designed to run freight trains over long distances, although they did occasionally carry passengers too. Their effectiveness was exemplified in 1983, when preserved engine 92203 Black Prince set the record for the heaviest train ever hauled by a steam locomotive in Britain, when it started a 2,162-ton train at the Foster Yeoman quarry in Somerset.

The 9Fs were the most powerful freight locomotives to run in the UK, and could be found throughout. Seen here pulling a large number of wagons is 92203 Black Prince.

Plenty of steam and lots of noise can be heard and seen as Black Prince builds up its maximum power to take its heavy wagon loads out of Toddington station.

SPECIFICATIONS

Class:	9F
Year:	1954
Wheel arrangement:	2-10-0
Cylinders:	2: 20 x 28 inch
Driving wheel diameter:	5 ft
Tractive effort:	39,670 lbs
Boiler pressure:	225 lbs
Valve gear:	Walschaerts
Coal capacity:	7 tons – 9 tons
Water capacity:	4,725 gallons – 5,625 gallons

Different designs were initially looked at by Riddles, but finally the 2-10-0 wheel configuration was decided on due to the increased traction and lower axle load that five coupled axles provided.

Design was carried out at Brighton, and the first engine went into service in 1954. A total of 251 locomotives were built between the Swindon and Crewe works, the last – 92220 – came out of Swindon in 1960 and was named Evening Star. Besides being the 999th standard steam locomotive to be built, it was also the last steam locomotive to be built by British Railways. Due to be given the regular BR freight black livery with no lining and the BR crest placed on the tender, this particular engine was adorned in BR

Withdrawals happened fairly quickly due to modernization plans, the first going in 1964, and just three years later the last was shipped off to the scrap yard. Several are now in preservation, including Evening Star.

92203 was the third 9F locomotive built by Swindon, in January 1959. When withdrawn, it was working the heavy iron ore trains out of Liverpool Docks to Shotton Steelworks, and it worked the

The Class 9F was the last in a series of standardized locomotive classes designed for British Railways during the 1950s, and was intended for use on fast, heavy freight trains over long distances.

Nine 9F locomotives have survived, with seven of them being rescued from Dai Woodham's scrap yard in Barry, South Wales. Two others were preserved upon withdrawal.

Brunswick Green – a colour that was normally reserved for prestigious express passenger locomotives. This series of locomotives was used as a type of test-bed, and several new ideas were tried, such as the Franco-Crosti boiler (numbers 92020-92029). Numbers 92165-92167 were built with a mechanical stoker, which was a helical screw that conveyed coal from the tender to the firebox. Few of these ideas were successful, but the one modification that did give some small benefit was the fitting of double blastpipes and chimneys, which allowed the engines to steam slightly more freely and thus generate higher power ranges.

92212 was one of the last 9Fs to be built, and in the final years of the Great Central route the 9Fs became the mainstay of the through freight workings from Annesley to Woodford.

last steam-hauled ore train in November 1967. Bought straight from BR, the locomotive was named 'Black Prince' by its new owner – however it never carried this name in service. It has since completed a thorough overhaul.

92212 came out of Swindon in September 1959, and was allocated the Somerset and Dorset route to Bournemouth. Several moves over the years saw it end its days at Carnforth. It was sent to scrap in January 1968, and was subsequently bought by 92212 Holdings Ltd. It moved to the Great Central Railway at Loughborough in September 1979, restoration was completed in September 1996, and the engine has been a regular performer in BR unlined black livery ever since.

Industrial Steam Locomotives

Industrial steam locomotives were not only with us at the start of the steam locomotive era, but they lasted right through to, and beyond, the end of steam, as it was described. When the modernization plans were unveiled in 1955 and all steam locomotives were planned to be withdrawn and shipped to the Barry scrap yard in South Wales, many of these powerful workhorses continued to carry out their duties behind the scenes.

Whether in a coal yard, at some power station or just shunting locomotives, these faithful engines were relied on to carry out their industrial work, with little fuss and mostly oblivious to the general public. From the coal mines of the North to the slate quarries of Wales and the tin mines of Cornwall, these faithful engines quietly went about their business.

Manufacturers like Manning Wardle, Andrew Barclay, Hunslet, Robert Heath, Hawthorne Leslie and, of course, Robert Stephenson, to name a few, all contributed their expertise and designs to create a fleet of engines that served the nation with pride. Here was a fleet of locomotives that worked tirelessly as back-up to the hard-worked locomotives that transported goods and passengers to all corners of Great Britain and beyond.

It is important that these locomotives, too, receive the praise they rightly deserve, and it is good to see that many have been saved into preservation, are lovingly restored and run on the many tracks now scattered around the country.

Shotton Colliery 0-6-0ST Stagshaw, a delightful Hawthorn Leslie saddle tank, pictured leaving East Tanfield station with its train of coaches. It is the classic UK industrial locomotive.

• HUNSLET

Since they started back in 1864, Hunslet have supplied industrial locomotives to countries all around the world. Over one hundred years later they supplied the last of 2,200 produced, to Java! Although this is recognized as the last British-built industrial steam locomotive, Hunslet continues to deliver a wide variety of innovative, high-quality products to a multitude of industries.

Back in 1864, a railway contractor and civil engineer, by the name of J. T. Leather, built up the company in the hope that his son would take an interest in the business and follow in his footsteps. Sadly it didn't happen.

Wimblebury is a good example of an Austerity saddle tank built by Hunslet of Leeds. It was delivered new in 1956 to the National Coal Board at Cannock Wood Colliery near Hednesford in Staffordshire, and worked there until it was withdrawn in the early 1970s.

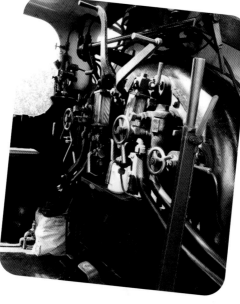

Built in 1902, Alice – Hunslet works 780 – worked at Dinorwic quarry, Wales, until about 1960, after which she was used for spare parts. Following restoration, she returned to steam in 1994 – having been rebuilt in the style of a quarry locomotive – cabless and with dumb buffers made from large lumps of timber. The locomotive moved back to the Bala Lake Railway, Wales, in 2003.

All the same, in the following years the company grew and became well known for their range of four- and six-coupled tank engines. During the early part of the 20th century the company, now officially Hunslet Engine Co. Ltd., started building bigger engines such as the series of 4-6-0Ts, which were for the War Department.

During 1927, their neighbour Manning Wardle went into liquidation and Hunslet purchased a considerable chunk of land from them to expand their business. As the 1930s progressed, so did the Great Depression, and with it Avonside Engine Company of Bristol closed, in 1934. The following year their business was purchased by Hunslet, complete with drawings, patterns and copyrights etc.

As the Second World War took hold, so Hunslet once again involved themselves with providing the Ministry of Supply with parts for artillery and aircraft components. Rail work also continued,

Built in 1909, the R & W Hawthorn locomotive Asbestos was delivered to the Turner & Newall Asbestos factory, Trafford Park, Manchester – hence its name.

with orders for a class of powerful six-coupled tank locomotives, which would become the famous 'Austerity' saddle tanks.

1938 saw another manufacturer collapse. This time it was Kitson & Co., who in fact had purchased the old Manning Wardle company when they went into receivership in 1927. Robert Stephenson and Hawthorns bought the Kitson outfit but sold the trade from those sources to Hunslet, increasing the workload even further. Hunslet also purchased the equity from Andrew Barclay & Co. Ltd. of Kilmarnock in 1972, which brought Scotland's sole remaining locomotive builder under the wing of the Hunslet group.

All the way up to the 21st century, Hunslet has maintained the standards that guaranteed its future, and make it one of the few remaining steam locomotive manufacturers in the UK.

• R & W HAWTHORN LESLIE AND COMPANY LIMITED

The company is generally referred to as Hawthorn Leslie, and was a St Peter's, Newcastle-upon-Tyne shipbuilding and locomotive manufacturer. The company got its name from the merger between the shipbuilder A. Leslie and Company and the locomotive works of R. and W. Hawthorn in 1870. The locomotive part of the business continued to manufacture engines, one of which was a 4-2-2-0 with four cylinders – two inside and two outside – connected separately to the two pairs of driving wheels. Further designs followed, many of which were exported around the world, and in 1937 the locomotive production part of the business was bought by their neighbours, Robert Stephenson and Company. With this they changed their name to Robert Stephenson and Hawthorns Ltd.

Bonnie Prince Charlie was built by Robert Stephenson and Hawthorns in 1951. She was used by Messrs. Coral on Poole Quay for shunting the gas works.

Robert Stephenson and Hawthorns 0-6-0 tank built at the Forth Bank Works in Newcastle-upon-Tyne in 1951. 7684 was delivered new to Meaford Power Station at Barlaston near Stone, and became 'MEA No. 2'.

• ROBERT STEPHENSON AND HAWTHORNS LTD (RSH)

The company was formed in September 1937, when Robert Stephenson and Company, based in Darlington, took over the loco-motive building department of Hawthorn Leslie, based in Newcastle. Robert Stephenson and Company – a locomotive manufacturing company and the first company set up specifically to build railway engines – was set up in 1823 in Forth Street, Newcastle-upon-Tyne, by George Stephenson, his son Robert, Edward Pease and Michael Longridge (the owner of the ironworks at Bedlington). It was founded as part of their construction of the Stockton and Darlington Railway, and its first engine was Locomotion No.1, which opened the line.

Seen double-heading with Asbestos is Bagnall 0-4-0, the very powerful but compact 15-inch, four-coupled saddle tank 2623 'Hawarden', built in 1940.

Prior to RSH becoming part of English Electric in 1955, they built a vast array of locomotives for both Britain and far-flung countries around the world. Locomotive building at the Newcastle-upon-Tyne works ended in 1961 and at Darlington in 1964.

• BAGNALL

The company was founded in 1875 by William Gordon Bagnall, and located at the Castle Engine works in Castle Town, Stafford.

Number 6 Douglas is an 0-4-0WT locomotive, built in 1918 by Andrew Barclay and Company Limited for the Airservice Construction Corps, and from 1921 until 1945 it worked at the RAF railway at Calshot Spit, Southampton.

The majority of their products were small four- and six-coupled steam locomotives for industrial use, many of which were narrow gauge. Bagnalls introduced several innovative forms of locomotive valve gear, including the Bagnall-Price and the Baguley. They also used marine (circular) fireboxes on narrow gauge engines. They ceased trading when they were taken over by English Electric Company Limited in 1962.

• ANDREW BARCLAY

In the first half of the 19th century, Ayrshire (Scotland) loom makers were hit hard by Thomas Morton's invention of the barrel loom, and so people had to seek other means of employment. Andrew Barclay was one of these people, and, as a way of moving away from the loom business, Barclay turned to the production of steam engines, opening his Kilmarnock works in 1840. This was a time when the railways were just beginning to boom, and his ability to manufacture locomotives to suit varying conditions and specifications enabled the company to expand rapidly, supplying engines overseas as well as to more local areas.

The company grew from its small beginnings and established the Caledonian Foundry and Engineering Works, still in Kilmarnock, and with this attracted many other related businesses to the area. One such company was the Glasgow and South Western Railway's locomotive and wagon building works at Bonnyton.

In the 1930s the engine manufacturing company of John Cochrane (Barrhead) Limited was bought out and, during the Second World War, the company was heavily involved with the production of parts for the army's Churchill and Valentine tanks.

During the 1950s, with the demise of steam engines advancing rapidly, the company began the manufacture of diesel engines, and

Andrew Barclay 0-4-0 saddle tank 2274 of 1949. NCB No.6 (North West Durham) area, delivered new to Springwell Bank Foot shed on the Bowes Railway, became Bowes 22. It was subsequently renumbered 85.

Number 2, 'Dolgoch', seen in its 1946 light green livery, was built in 1866 by Fletcher, Jennings and Company. This 0-4-0 tank engine has a back tank (behind the cab) and a well tank (between the frames).

in 1963 it acquired the goodwill of the North British Locomotive Company, Glasgow. The company was noted for constructing simple and robust locomotives, and became the largest builder of fireless locomotives in Britain, building 114 of them between 1913 and 1961.

However, in 1972 the company itself was acquired by the Leeds-based Hunslet Group of companies, and its name was changed in 1989 to Hunslet-Barclay Limited. The locomotive interests of Hunslet-Barclay were bought by the LH Group, Staffordshire, with Hunslet-Barclay at Kilmarnock continuing in the business of design, manufacture and refurbishment of multiple units, rolling stock,

bogies and wheel sets. In November 2007, Hunslet-Barclay was bought by the locomotive builder Brush Traction of Loughborough, and re-named Brush-Barclay.

Originally built in 1864 by Fletcher, Jennings & Co. of Whitehaven as a 0-4-0ST, 'Talyllyn' had a short wheelbase and long rear overhang, which led to its rapid conversion to an 0-4-2ST.

• FLETCHER, JENNINGS

Fletcher, Jennings & Co. was an engineering concern based at Lowca near Whitehaven in Cumbria, England. They took over the business of Tulk and Ley in 1857 and concentrated on four- and six-coupled industrial tank locomotives from then until 1884. By this time, nearly two hundred locomotives had been built, and the company acquired limited liability as Lowca Engineering Company Limited.

In 1905, the name was changed to New Lowca Engineering Company Limited, but orders had declined rapidly and the company also suffered a disastrous fire – all production ceased, and it was finally wound up in 1927.

Sir Berkeley, built in Leeds in December 1890 as Manning, Wardle & Company's works number 1210, was supplied new to Messrs. Logan & Hemingway, a firm of railway-related engineering contractors.

• MANNING WARDLE

Manning Wardle & Company, established in 1840, located their Boyne Engine Works in Jack Lane in the Hunslet district of Leeds, West Yorkshire. No stranger to the locomotive building industry, Leeds had seen the earliest builder, Matthew Murray, manufacture the first commercially successful steam locomotive, Salamanca, in Holbeck in 1812. By 1856 several manufacturers had set up business there, the most notable being E. B. Wilson and Company, but they found times difficult, and by 1858 they had gone out of business, with Manning Wardle purchasing the company designs.

It wasn't long before two other companies also moved to Jack Lane – Hunslet Engine Company and Hudswell, Clarke & Company – and the competition between all three was strong, although Manning Wardle did manufacture engines that differed from those of the other two companies. They concentrated mainly on specialized locomotives for contractor's use, building up a range of engines suitable for all types of contracting work, and many of their standard gauge and a variety of narrow gauge locomotives were exported around the world.

The company used traditional manufacturing methods and failed to capitalize on the mass production techniques being used by the other manufacturers. This made them uncompetitive, and it wasn't

too long before this took effect, leaving them to close down in 1927 after building over 2,000 steam locomotives.

After closure, the drawings, designs and equipment were acquired by Kitsons, who manufactured 23 Manning Wardle-designed engines, but who then also closed in 1938. The patterns then passed to Robert Stephenson and Hawthorns, who built a further five locomotives of the Manning Wardle design.

• ROBERT HEATH & SONS
Robert Heath & Sons were well-known Staffordshire ironmasters, at one time reputed to be the largest producers of bar iron in the world. Furnaces, forges and mills were operated at Black Bull, Biddulph and Ford Green, together with collieries and a network of private railway lines.

Robert Heath 0-4-0 saddle tank-built 1885. One of the real unique gems of the steam collection at Foxfield, this is a thoroughly local engine and a very remarkable survivor. Robert Heath & Sons were well known local ironmasters, at one time reputed to be the largest producers of bar iron in the world.

Fairlie 0-4-4-0T 'Earl of Merioneth', built by the Ffestiniog Railway Company Boston Lodge Works in 1979, is pictured here approaching Blaenau Ffestiniog with the up train from Porthmadog, Wales.

Heath's not only bought locomotives, they also made their own. The original source of the design of Heath's four-wheeled locomotives appears to be one bought new from Falcon of Loughborough in 1885, though little is known about the locomotive fleet at that time. It seems that Heath's set to work to copy it, of which number 6 was the first. Heath's went on to build a further eleven four-wheeled locomotives up until the First World War, which were gradually modified and re-built over the years. In addition, two six-wheeled locomotives were built in 1915 and 1924, based on a much re-built locomotive originally delivered by Black Hawthorn in 1888.

After the First World War, Heath's amalgamated with the Low Moor Company, iron makers of Bradford, and by the late 1920s the iron side of the business was in financial trouble.

• FAIRLIE

The Fairlie was invented and patented by the Scottish engineer Robert F. Fairlie in 1864. In 1869 Fairlie's company built a locomotive named 'Little Wonder' for the Ffestiniog Railway, a slate hauler in North Wales, which proved to be an outstanding success. Fairlie gave the Ffestiniog Railway Company a perpetual licence to use the Fairlie patent without restriction, in return for using the line

and the success of its Fairlie locomotives in his publicity. Locomotive production ceased at the end of 1870, but the Fairlie Engine & Rolling Stock Company continued as an office for design and for the licensing of Fairlie locomotive manufacture.

• KERR STUART

Founded in Glasgow, Scotland in 1881 by James Kerr, as James Kerr & Co., the company became Kerr, Stuart & Co. from 1883 when John Stuart was taken on as a partner. They bought Hartley, Arnoux and Fanning in 1892 and moved into the California Works in Stoke to begin building all their own locomotives. Kerr Stuart designs are typified by having a single trailing truck – allowing a large firebox to be placed behind the driving wheels – and/or having a saddle tank.

In the late 1920s a number of diesel locomotives were built which were very successful. However, further development was stopped when Kerr Stuart went into receivership, and the firm's goodwill (designs, spare parts etc) was bought by the Hunslet Engine Company.

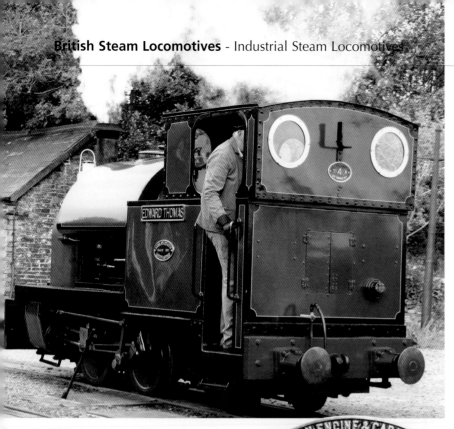

• FALCON ENGINE & CAR WORKS LTD

In 1865 Henry Hughes, a timber merchant engineer, began building horse-drawn tramcars and railway rolling stock at the Falcon Works in Loughborough. It seems that his company, Hughes's Locomotive & Tramway Engine Works Ltd began producing steam loco-motives in about 1867 for the Paris exhibition. Among the first steam locomotives was 'Belmont', which ran on the Snailbeach District Railways. Three 2 ft 3 in (686 mm) gauge 0-4-0STs for the Corris Railway were supplied in 1878.

In 1881 they built two 3 ft (914 mm) gauge 0-4-0STs for the Liverpool Corporation Water Committee, but in 1881 the company ran into legal problems, and in 1882 was in receivership.

Late in 1882 it reformed as Falcon Engine & Car Works Ltd, and supplied three more same-design locomotives for the railways at Vyrnwy. It seems that the factory remained busy with both railway and tramway locomotives and rolling stock, including tank locomotives. 1889 saw assets taken over by the Anglo-American Brush Electric Light Corporation.

Edward Thomas is a 0-4-2ST narrow gauge locomotive that was built in 1921 by Kerr, Stuart & Co. Ltd for use on the Corris Railway. It was purchased by the Talyllyn railway in Wales in 1951, and named after their former manager.

Sir Handel, shown here, is a fictional locomotive from The Railway Series by Rev. W. Awdry and its adaptation TV series, Thomas the Tank Engine and Friends. Sir Handel lives and works on the Skarloey Railway on the Island of Sodor as Engine No. 3. Based on the locomotive Sir Haydn, which works at the Talyllyn Railway in Wales, it was built by Henry Hughes & Co. at the Falcon Works in Loughborough in 1878.

Glossary of Terms

Ash Pan - This is found below the firebox of a steam locomotive to catch the hot ashes falling from the grate.

Automatic Train Control - (ATC) An early system invented by the Great Western Railway in 1910 to give drivers an audio warning of the status of the signal ahead.

Auto-train - A locomotive-powered train which can be driven with the locomotive either pulling or pushing the coaches. When pushing coaches, the train is driven from a special compartment at the front of the leading coach, where some of the driving controls are duplicated.

Axle Weight - The weight carried on any axle of a train.

Back Plate - The inner plate of the back of a steam locomotive firebox.

Belpaire Fireboxes - These had a bottom narrow enough to fit between the frames of a locomotive. They widened higher up to the width of the barrel, thus providing a larger steam space and greater water surface area in the hottest part of the boiler.

Blast-Pipe - Exhaust steam is released from the cylinders via the blast-pipe located inside the smoke-box.

BR - British Rail. Ran the British Railway system between 1948 and 1993.

Branch Line - A railway route which branches off a main through route at one end, and usually finishes at a terminus at the other end.

Broad Gauge - A railway line laid to a gauge significantly wider than standard gauge.

Bulleid Valve Gear - A steam locomotive valve gear, which in principle is similar to Walschaerts valve gear, but where the combination lever and eccentric rod are driven by chains from the driving axle.

Bunker - The coal space, usually at the front of the tender, or just behind the cab of tank engines.

Caprotti Valve Gear - Invented by the Italian engineer Arturo Caprotti – a type of steam locomotive valve gear utilizing poppet type valves.

Compound Engine - To maximize efficiency on steam locomotives, some were designed to use steam at high pressure in one or more cylinders. Exhaust steam from those cylinders then drove other low-pressure cylinders before finally being exhausted to atmosphere.

Corridor Tender - A tender incorporating a passageway through it and a corridor connection to the coaches to which it might be attached.

Dome - A dome-shaped protrusion on the top of a steam locomotive boiler. Typically this conceals the steam collection pipe for the regulator, which needs to be at the highest point of the boiler to minimize the chances of priming. Domes may also be used for other purposes.

Double Header - A train which is hauled by two locomotives coupled together.

Down Line - The line on a multi-track main line where the direction of travel is away from the major city.

Driving Wheel - The wheels which actually drive the vehicle along. In the case of a steam engine, these will be the large wheels in the middle of the locomotive connected together by coupling rods.

Dynamometer Car - A railway vehicle which incorporates instruments for measuring draw-bar pull, speed, and work carried out by a locomotive to which it is coupled.

Fairlie - A steam locomotive with a boiler having two barrels connected to a common firebox mounted on the mainframe. The cab is in the middle and a power bogie is located under each boiler.

Fire Tube - Boiler tubes through which hot gases from the fire pass.

Firebox - Literally a box containing the fire. It is surrounded by water on the top and all sides. The bottom is a grate with an ash pan below that.

Fireless steam locomotives - Similar to a conventional steam locomotive but has a reservoir (known as a steam accumulator) instead of a boiler. This reservoir is part-filled with water and charged with steam from a stationary boiler. The locomotive can then work on the stored steam until the pressure has dropped to a minimum level, after which it must be re-charged.

Footplate - The floor of a locomotive cab.

Gooch Valve Gear - A valve gear similar to Stephenson valve gear, but with the expansion link fixed so that it may pivot only. Drive from the expansion link to the valve spindle is taken via a radius link which may be moved up and down in the expansion link to obtain reversal.

Goods Shed - A building through or alongside which a railway track and a roadway passes, and which incorporates storage facilities. Such sheds are used for the loading and unloading of goods between road and railway vehicles.

Gresley Valve Gear - A type of conjugated valve gear used extensively on locomotives designed by Sir Nigel Gresley of the London North Eastern Railway.

GWR - Great Western Railway.

Inside Cylinders - Steam locomotive cylinders which are located between the frames.

Inside Frames - A vehicle frame which is entirely located between the wheels.

Inside Valve Gear - A steam locomotive valve gear which is entirely located between the frames.

Kylchap Blast-Pipe - A type of steam locomotive blast-pipe in which the steam jet is split into four streams, and then passed into the chimney via a petticoat pipe divided into four parts.

Leading Wheels - Locomotive carryingwheels which are forward of the driven wheels.

LMS - London Midland and Scottish Railway.

LNER - London North Eastern Railway

Locomotive Works - A factory or depot where locomotives are built and overhauled.

Main Line - A railway route interconnecting locations of major importance.

Mile Post - A line-side post on which is printed the distance in miles from a datum point.

Mixed Train - A train consisting of a mixture of passenger and goods stock.

Motion - A general term for driving and valve gear on steam locomotives.

Narrow Gauge - Any railway of less than the UK standard gauge of 4 ft 8½ in. Commonly used for industrial sites and particularly in Wales for use in and around slate mines.

Outside Cylinders - Steam locomotive cylinders which are secured on the outside of the frame.

Outside Frames - Vehicle frames, the sides of which are outside the wheels.

Outside Valve Gear - Steam locomotive valve gear which is located outside the frame.

Pannier Tank - Pannier tanks are hung on the sides of the boiler of a steam locomotive to carry the required water supply.

Push-Pull Train - Another term for an auto-train.

Rail Car/Rail Motor - A self-propelled railway coach. This term is sometimes used to refer to an auto-train.

Rocking Grate - A grate consisting of small sections which can be rocked to shake the remains of the fire through into the ash pan after the finish of a days work. Most steam locomotives have a flat grate which has to be raked out by hand via the fire-hole. Rocking grates require much less effort.

Rolling Stock - Railway vehicles which are not self-propelled.

Saddle Tank - A steam locomotive which carries its water in tanks draped over the boiler barrel like a saddle.

Shunter - A locomotive used for moving or rearranging rolling stock within the bounds of a station or goods yard.

Smoke Deflectors - Large boilers have short chimneys, and smoke therefore tends to blow back along the side of the boiler, obscuring the driver's vision. Large plates fixed alongside the smoke-box act to deflect the smoke upwards clear of the cab windows.

Smoke-Box - A cylindrical drum on the front of a steam locomotive boiler, into which the hot gases from the boiler tubes pass. By routing the exhaust steam from the cylinders through a blast pipe within the smoke-box and directing the resulting jet out the chimney, a partial vacuum is created in the smoke-box, and by making it as large as possible, a more even draught is created over the area of the tubes. This vacuum draws the hot gases from the fire through the boiler tubes, thus heating the boiler water more rapidly and producing more steam to replace that used.

SR - Southern Railway.

Standard Gauge - The UK standard gauge is 4 ft 8½ in. Anything wider is referred to as broad gauge, and anything narrower as narrow gauge.

Steam Dome - A dome-shaped protrusion on top of a steam locomotive boiler, inside which the steam-collection pipe is located.

Stephenson Valve Gear - A steam engine valve gear which is usually located between the mainframes of a locomotive. Motion is taken from two eccentrics secured to one of the driving axles. From these, two rods (the eccentric rods) are connected to either end of a link (the expansion link), which is thus oscillated. Movement of the valve spindle is taken from a die block which is free to slide within the expansion link. Reversal is carried out by moving the expansion link bodily, so that the die block takes up a new position at the other end of its slide.

Superheating - Steam taken directly from a boiler retains the same temperature and pressure as when it was produced, and is said to be 'saturated'. By taking such steam and heating it further, a much greater volume of gas can be produced for a small amount of extra heat. Tests have shown that superheating can result in a 25 per cent economy in coal and 30 per cent in water. Introduced in the 1900s and used mainly on the larger main-line engines. Superheated steam will always be dry.

Tank Locomotive - A steam locomotive that carries its own water supply, rather than towing a separate vehicle for the purpose.

Tender - A railway vehicle which is permanently coupled to a steam locomotive, and in which water and fuel are carried.

Tender Locomotive - A steam locomotive that carries its water supply and coal in a tender.

Throat Plate A downward extension of the front of a locomotive firebox below the boiler barrel.

Top Feed - Some, mainly earlier, designs of steam locomotive fed water to the boiler from the sides or bottom. This resulted in localized cooling and unequal contraction of boiler plates. Many later designs used top feed, which fed water through the boiler top on to shallow trays; the water would thus be heated before coming into contact with boiler parts.

Tractive Effort - A calculated mean draw-bar-pull which a locomotive could exert when working at maximum capacity. Frictional losses in the locomotive itself and its tender (if any) are neglected when formulating tractive effort.

Trailing Wheels - Locomotive carrying-wheels which are in the rear of the driven wheels.

Train Shed - That area of a railway station in which the platforms and tracks are under the cover of a roofed structure.

Up Line - That line of a multi-track main line where the direction of travel is towards the major city.

Valve Gear - The system of rods and cranks which connect the pistons and valves to the wheels and controls the admission of steam to the cylinders.

Walschaerts Valve Gear - A steam engine valve gear used extensively on outside-cylindered locomotives. One component of motion is taken from an eccentric or return crank secured to one of the driving axles at approximately 90° to the main crank. From this a rod (eccentric rod) transfers movement to one end of a centre-pivoted link (radius link), which is thus oscillated. Movement is then taken from a die block that is free to slide within the radius link via a rod (radius rod) to one end of a lever (combination lever). The combination lever combines the movement of the radius rod with that of the cross head via a union link connected to the other end of the combination lever. The combined movement is transferred to the valve spindle via a third connection on the combination lever near the end connected to the radius rod. Reversal is carried out by moving the radius rod so the die block takes up a new position at the other end of the slide.

Water Column - A device consisting of a vertical tube from which a flexible hose hangs. The device is used for filling the water tanks of locomotives.

Index

Acknowledgements

The author would like to thank all the many Preserved
Railways, their informative websites and their personnel, who
gladly helped with information and who voluntarily give their
time to keep our fond memories alive. They work tirelessly
to run these magnificent locomotives for our pleasure.
Thanks must also go to the owners of these glorious smoking
giants, who take pride in allowing us to see and experience
the way life used to be when steam ruled the rails.

Due to the historical nature of the subject, it was necessary
to research much of the information from many different
sources, both on the Internet and from my local library.
I would like to thank all these sources of which there
are far too many to list, but which are well known
to locomotive enthusiasts.

FOOTNOTE:

*It has been argued that the initials LMSR should be used
to be consistent with LNER, GWR and SR. However the
London, Midland and Scottish Railway's corporate image
used LMS, and this is what is generally used in historical
circles. The LMS occasionally also used the initials LM&SR.
For consistency, we have in general used the initials LMS.*

*It should be noted that due to age and inconsistent
information, some figures given for the locomotives
featured in this book may be subject to discussion.
In every case we have attempted to give the correct
information, but we apologize for any statement
that may be misleading or incorrect.*